TEACHING SERMONS
SECOND SERIES: OLD TESTAMENT

D0492456

By the same Author:

THE ASCETIC WORKS OF ST BASIL
CHICHESTER CATHEDRAL, ITS HISTORY AND ART
CONCISE BIBLE COMMENTARY
DIVINE HUMANITY
EIGHTEENTH CENTURY PIETY
A HISTORY OF THE S.P.C.K.
TEACHING SERMONS (First Series)
GOOD FRIDAY (Ed.)
LITURGY AND WORSHIP (Ed.)

TEACHING SERMONS

Second Series

OLD TESTAMENT

by

W. K. LOWTHER CLARKE, D.D.

LONDON

S · P · C · K

1961

First published in 1961
by S.P.C.K.
Holy Trinity Church
Marylebone Road
London N.W.1

Printed in Great Britain by
The Talbot Press (S.P.C.K.)
Saffron Walden, Essex

© W. K. Lowther Clarke, 1961

Contents

Preface

In 1942 a book of mine was published with the title *Teaching Sermons*, containing a short discourse for every Sunday of the year. Encouraged by its reception I have written a successor, on different lines. For many years I have taught the Old Testament with a view to examinations and have wanted an opportunity to give a more pastoral turn to my teaching than was possible in academic lectures. Also I have felt that there might be an opening for a book of sermons on the Old Testament as a guide to Lay Readers, who often have little chance of knowing how critical study has enriched our understanding of the Bible. The emotional side of a sermon and its practical application to modern needs are hardly represented in this book. On the basis of the help given here a preacher should be able to supply what is lacking. Nearly all the sermons have been preached in the course of a long ministry, but a few have been specially written.

While there is nothing consciously denominational in this book I naturally write as an Anglican. In our Church sermons are expected to be short. Also with our constant use of the Psalms, and our lessons taken from the Old Testament, there is probably a special need for our congregations to hear Old Testament sermons. The subjects of this book are arranged more or less in the order of the Hebrew Bible.

W.K.L.C.

1

Creation

And God said, Let there be light: and there was light.

GENESIS 1. 3.

THE MAJESTIC story of Creation will be our subject to-day. Nothing need be said about modern science; what the Bible teaches will be enough for us.

As you know, Genesis has two accounts of Creation, widely different. In chapter 2 there is a charming piece of folk-lore; myth if you like, but you must remember that certain truths are best conveyed in story form, especially for children, and that the minds of the early Hebrews were in some respects like those of children. The other, and later, story in chapter 1 comes to terms with the science of the day and with matchless dignity and skill proclaims eternal truths. Let us begin with the early account, which tells of the garden of Eden and its inhabitants.

The story was probably written down about 900 B.C. but will have been told long before; it will have been familiar to David a hundred years earlier. Man is made first, before the animals. The Lord takes the dust of the ground and shapes it to the required form and then breathes life into the figure he has made. The description is derived from the work of the potter, forming a jug or dish out of clay. It is a very good way of describing Creation: the potter has in his mind the idea of what he intends to make and he models the clay accordingly; but God gives life, flowing out from his own life as he breathes into the lifeless mass. Then the Lord makes the animals, which are brought to Adam—the word means humanity. Adam is at home with Nature and is friendly with the beasts, but none of them meets his needs. So the Lord creates woman, taking a rib out of Adam, who has first been cast into a deep sleep. (When anaesthetics were first used at childbirth, old-fashioned people were disturbed; the method was unnatural. They were told to read Genesis, where the Almighty gives Adam an anaesthetic before his operation.) The word Eve means "life", and the story is clearly meant to be symbolical. Notice the delicate treatment of sex. Man as originally created is humanity, consisting of female as well as male, and then for the purpose of life in this world the sexes are differentiated. In *that* world, where they "neither marry nor are given in marriage", man will revert to the original purpose of the Creator, and the characteristic excellences of man and woman will be merged in one "new man".

Now let us turn to Genesis 1, which was probably written down in Babylonia some 500 years before Christ. The Hebrews were familiar with the ideas held by the Gentiles. Everything began with a battle of the gods. Tiamat, the great deep, rose in rebellion against the other gods, and Marduk was deputed to deal with her. Finally Marduk divided Tiamat into two parts, one forming the sea and the underground waters from which come the springs, the other being stored away in the sky to provide rain. The origin of the myth is obvious. The two great rivers of Mesopotamia, Euphrates and Tigris, often overflow and cause floods; they are the enemies of God and man unless they are controlled. Also they deposit silt at the mouth of the Persian Gulf, and the early inhabitants of that district kept seeing dry land appear. The Bible writer takes the story and remodels it to teach precious truths. There is no primeval struggle: all goes back to the fiat of the Almighty God of the Hebrews. "Let there be light: and there was light." "He spake, and it was done."

Out of primeval chaos order appears. The first task in Creation is to deal with the unruly waters, which are divided, part forming the sea, part being put in the sky. Yes, says the writer, things were ordered aright—but not by Marduk. Our God did it by his mere word. Then God said, "Let the dry land appear", as the Babylonians had seen it appear. We pass on to the fourth day, remembering that the Babylonians worshipped the sun, moon, and stars. *God* made the sun to rule the day, the moon to rule the night; that is all. True, they are useful to fix the calendar, but faced with the elaborate apparatus of star-worship the Bible merely says, "He made the stars also".

The sixth day witnessed the creation of man: "Let us make man in our image", a rational being who can have communion with God, the crown of creation, ruling over the animals. And we have the same lesson as in the other story. God made Man, that is humanity, "male and female created he them."

While the Bible was never meant to teach us science, there is singularly little in the story to clash with the conclusions of modern science. In both, man is the crown of creation; there is no reason to think that dogs or horses might make an evolutionary jump and surpass him. The whole process is the result of a plan, not a purposeless accident. Science is built up on a belief in the orderly working of Nature, though it may prefer not to use the word "God". And, "God saw everything that he had made, and behold it was very good". The wonders of scientific discovery are the fulfilment of God's command to "subdue the earth". Man learns to conquer Nature by obeying her. A vastly increased power is now put into the hands of man; the secrets of the atom are part of the world which God made and found very good. The peril of the present situation lies not in Nature but in man's misuse of Nature.

We conclude that, while the outward form of the Creation story is conditioned by the surroundings of the ancient Near East, the underlying truths are of divine origin. You have only to compare the story with the beliefs held by other nations to realize this and to thank God for such a noble and inspiring account of the beginning of things.

2

Adam and Eve

The woman . . . gave me of the tree, and I did eat.
GENESIS 3. 12.

SOMETIMES PREACHERS have waxed eloquent about the perfections of the first man. Thus Robert South, a seventeenth-century divine, said: "An Aristotle was but the rubbish of an Adam, and Athens but the rudiments of Paradise." The Bible is more modest in its description. Adam and Eve are naked, and their first clothes, after the fig leaves, are made of animals' skins. They live on fruit, and the arts and crafts are still in the future. But they are unmistakably man and woman, like ourselves, and the inward struggle between sin and conscience has never been told better than in this immortal parable.

How did sin come into the world? As it comes to each of us in childhood, by disobedience and the assertion of self-will. St Augustine in a famous passage of his Confessions describes a sin of boyhood, when he robbed an orchard of pears, not because he particularly wanted the pears but for fun, and because it was forbidden. (I am afraid we have a less tender conscience when we look back on the peccadilloes of our childhood.) Adam knows perfectly well that one tree in the

4

garden bears forbidden fruit, but he doubts God's wisdom in making this particular prohibition. It will do me good, he says; I shall enlarge my experience and gain knowledge of good and evil. Or, as we say, I will try anything once. But when he has eaten, conscience wakes up—why did I do it? So he thinks of excuses. I know, it was Eve's fault; so he puts the blame on the woman, setting an example for all men in time to come. Also, he and Eve try to hide from God. How true to life it is! Children especially are ready to shift the blame on to "the other boys", and little children have been known to hide when they have done wrong. Even dogs, copying the ways of the human beings with whom they live, have a rudimentary sense of guilt and will hide from their masters when they have erred. Adam and Eve, having lost their first innocence, develop a sense of shame in other ways, realizing for the first time that they are naked.

So far we have said nothing about the serpent. His part in the story is to teach that evil comes from outside into the world that God saw to be good. To identify him with the devil is natural, but curiously enough there is no reference to this chapter elsewhere in the Old Testament, and not until the book of Wisdom, written perhaps a hundred years before Christ, is the identification made. The story is interested in man and his free will, which makes possible both his splendid achievements and his woeful fall; the serpent is of secondary importance.

When God banishes Adam and Eve from Eden he says that another and worse sin is looming ahead; they might eat of the tree of life and live for ever. In other words, the root sin for man is pride, desire to be like God, to despise God's holy law, thinking he knows better. One detail in the story must not be overlooked. Eve was overcome by the beauty of the fruit; "it was a delight to the eyes". Moralists might say that this is a characteristic feminine weakness, especially where clothes are concerned. Genesis doesn't say it in so many

5

words but perhaps thinks that Adam went too far in wanting to please his wife.

The story ends with expulsion from Paradise, and Adam and Eve tackling the hardships of life in the world as we know it. The fall of man in one sense was the ascent of man. A lotus-eating existence in a lovely garden could not have satisfied the noblest elements in human nature. But that is a problem outside the scope of the story.

As I have said, the chapter stands alone in the Old Testament; not until the New Testament does it come into its own. There we find it profoundly influencing the mind of St Paul. Two passages will be enough to quote.

First, the great doctrinal hymn of Philippians, chapter 2. Christ, "being in the form of God, counted it not a prize to be on an equality with God" but "humbled (denied) himself". The first Adam indulged himself, the Second Adam denied himself. The first Adam would have grasped at the prize of equality with God, the Second Adam renounced it.

The second passage is Romans, chapter 7, where Paul is often thought to be telling his own experiences. In a sense they are his, but they are the experiences of all men, beginning with Adam. He is meditating on the story of the garden of Eden. "Sin, finding occasion through the commandment, beguiled me"—as the forbidden fruit first led Adam into sin, just because it was forbidden. "Sin becoming death to me through that which was good"—the fruit was good, being God's creation, and the commandment not to touch was of course good. Then in a sense he excuses himself, like Adam: "So now it is no more I that do it, but sin which dwells in me. . . . I delight in the law of God after the inward man, but I see a different law in my members, warring against the law of my mind." Then he cries in despair: "Who shall deliver me out of this body which brings death?" and gets the assurance of salvation in Christ.

3

The Flood

I do bring a flood of waters upon the earth, to destroy all flesh. GENESIS 6. 17.

CHILDHOOD MEMORIES of Noah's Ark and the eight unshapely human figures that went with the animals make it hard for us to take the story seriously. Our forefathers in the Middle Ages felt the same, for in the mystery plays Noah's wife provided comic relief, refusing to enter the Ark and having to be pushed in amid shouts of laughter. But nevertheless let us try to understand the story as the Bible writers did.

There are two landmarks in the history of scholars' understanding the outward features of the narrative, as opposed to its inner meaning. First in 1872 George Smith, an assistant in the British Museum, who had for years been working at the task of repairing some 25,000 clay tablets with Assyrian (cuneiform) inscriptions, read a paper at a meeting, in which he gave the Assyrian story of the Flood. Part was missing, but enough remained to prove its remarkable resemblance to the Bible account. Other tablets dealing with the same subject were soon found, and it became clear that the story had been told in these terms 4,000 or even 5,000 to 6,000 years ago. Even the raven and the dove are found in the Assyrian story. The other landmark was the recent discovery at Ur of the Chaldees, in the south of Mesopotamia, of a deposit seven to eight feet thick, clearly the silt left by a great flood. Similar finds have been made elsewhere in Iraq, not apparently belonging to the same period. There must have been several floods, one of them so extensive that it became the basis of a saga, which Abraham may well have brought with him when he left Mesopotamia in search of the promised land.

7

Why should the Bible attach so much importance to a flood that devastated a large part of Mesopotamia? There must be some hidden meaning. We go back in thought to ancient Egypt and Babylonia. In Egypt Pharaoh was held to be divine, because he first had given peace and succeeded in regulating the waters of the Nile, so that all could get their share of the yearly overflow and be able to grow crops. In Mesopotamia there was in early times no strong central government, and the great rivers, always erratic, were not controlled in the same way. From time to time dreadful floods occurred, wiping out whole cities. Water came to be regarded as a hostile power, useful indeed when controlled but liable to do untold damage. So the old Babylonian myth arose, in which Tiamat, the goddess of the great deep, rebelled against the gods, who deputed Marduk, one of their number, to put her down. This comes in the Babylonian story of Creation, in which Tiamat is divided into two parts, one the sea and the underground sources of the springs, the other the clouds in the sky. An echo of this is found in Genesis 1, where the waters under the earth are divided from those above the firmament. Now this motif recurs in the story of the Flood. When Noah had entered the Ark, "all the fountains of the great deep were broken up, and the windows of heaven were opened". The primeval forces of destruction, hitherto kept under control, are allowed to wreak vengeance on a guilty generation. *But they are still under control.* They come into operation at the word of God, and when they have done their work they return to their original place.

Noah and his family stand for the faithful remnant; the Ark has always been taken to symbolize the Church, where the faithful remain in safety during the outbreak of evil. In Christian symbolism the waters of the Flood have been taken to represent baptism, in which through water the convert enters the Church; though that does not fit in with the more

8

natural meaning of purification and washing, where water is a good, not a bad, thing.

The end of the story is very important. Noah and his family emerge from the Ark and Noah offers sacrifice, which is accepted by God. Then God makes a new covenant with the human race, of which the rainbow is the outward sign. In stormy weather the rainbow assures us that the sun is shining all the time, and not far away from us. We are taught therefore that the forces of evil, for which the Flood stands, will not prevail. There will always be evil in the world, but never so much and so strong as to overcome the good.

Further, the covenant is made with Shem, Ham, and Japheth. According to the Bible, Shem was the father of the Semitic races, of which Israel is one. Ham and Japheth were the fathers of all the rest. The commandment forbidding murder, "Whoso sheddeth man's blood, by man shall his blood be shed" (9. 6), is given to the whole human race. The covenant includes the Gentiles. "These three were the sons of Noah: and of these was the whole earth overspread" (9. 19). This is the foundation of natural religion and justifies us in trying to find something of the original revelation in heathen religions. What is even more remarkable, the covenant is with Nature as well as man: "The covenant which I make between me and you and every living creature that is with you." The harmony of Adam and the animals in Paradise is restored; man is elder brother to the beasts and a trustee for their welfare, responsible to God for his stewardship.

9

4

The Tower of Babel

Let us build us . . . a tower whose top may reach unto heaven. GENESIS 11. 4.

WHAT A charming text, reminding us of our childhood, when we sat on the floor and tried to build a tall tower with our bricks.

The very remarkable story of the Tower of Babylon stands alone in the Bible, for there is no reference to it elsewhere. The ordinary interpretation is that mankind, having memories of the Flood, played for safety by building a house high enough to be beyond the reach of any flood. Or else that men were trying to storm heaven and so provoked God's wrath. The Hebrew writer sees in the story an explanation of how differences in language arose; but this is very forced. Babel (Babylon) suggested to him the Hebrew word *bālăl*, which means "confound". But this is only a kind of pun. *Babel* cannot mean *bālăl*. As a matter of fact it means "gate of God", which suggests a very different explanation.

Let us first look at the beginning of the story, which tells of the building of a *ziggurat*. Now what does that mean? *Ziggurat* is the Babylonian word for a special kind of tower, which was introduced into Mesopotamia by the first inhabitants of whom we have any record, the Sumerians, who probably came from the mountainous land of Persia. There can be no doubt that, accustomed to sanctuaries on hills, they represented the high and holy places they had known by artificial towers. Some thirty-three of these *ziggurats* have been discovered in Mesopotamia, or at least remains of them, if only the foundations. The best preserved is that at Ur of the Chaldees, where an artificial mound was found to contain the lower part of a *ziggurat*, with three great staircases

10

leading up to it. But we know more about the *ziggurat* of Babylon, of which only the foundations remain. It was of immense size, the lower stage being 300 feet square and the top rising to a height of nearly 300 feet. When it was built is not known, but by the time of Nabopolassar, father of Nebuchadnezzar, it had fallen into disrepair and had to be rebuilt. The baked bricks, and bitumen to act as mortar, have been discovered, as described in the Bible. Nabopolassar tells how he took off his royal robes and carried bricks and earth on his head. "As for Nebuchadnezzar, my first-born son, the beloved of my heart, I made him bear the mortar, the offerings of wine and oil, in company with my subjects." It is fascinating to think of the terrible Nebuchadnezzar of the Bible working as a labourer in the cause of religion.

This *ziggurat* had apparently seven storeys, each smaller than the last, and on the narrow top storey was built a temple. Herodotus the historian, who with his eager Greek curiosity visited Babylon, says that a spiral staircase led all the way up to the top, where was a temple, in which was no idol. Surely we recognize this staircase reaching up to heaven, for the *ziggurat* suggested Jacob's dream of a ladder leading from earth to heaven, with God's messengers going up and down. This must have been the original purpose of the tower, to make a glorious abode for the God of heaven.

Now there are two ways of explaining the moral of the story. First, it is a judgement on human pride. "The best laid schemes of mice and men gang aft agley", says Burns. This is just the verdict we should expect from the Hebrews, for whom Babylon meant the haughty oppressor. Reports will have reached them of the ruinous state of the famous tower, before the great restoration. And the judgement they passed is true enough. God does bring to nought many of our plans, conceived without his guidance. How we looked forward to peace and planned for it during the war! And how disappointing peace proved when it came! The old League of

11

Nations, initiated by President Wilson, was ruined when the United States refused to join and before the second war broke out had become a fiasco. The Welfare State, hailed by many as a clear case of applied Christianity, has already begun to show cracks and strains. The confusion of tongues with which the story of Babel ends recalls to us the problem of to-day, when nations agree on terms but understand them differently. "Democracy" means something very different in Russia and the English-speaking countries. I hasten to add that, if our good turns to evil, God overrules our evil by his good. "There is some soul of goodness in things evil", as Shakespeare says (*Henry V*).

But the story has another lesson which I find attractive. Here is an early people, outside the circle of direct revelation, who with all their gross superstitions are reaching out and up to God. Using all their resources they build a splendid shrine for their God, exalted on high far above the city. The staircase is for men, or at least a few privileged ones, to approach to God, and for God, lodged in his temple, to come down and dwell among the people. Truly "God left not himself without witness". In due course the tower fell, like all other human achievements, but the story proclaims its ancient lesson, "for the word of the Lord endureth for ever".

5

Father of the Faithful

By faith Abraham . . . went out, not knowing whither he went. HEBREWS 11. 8.

THE GREAT figure of Abraham, Father of the Faithful, looms in the past of three religions—Christianity, Judaism, and Islam. With him sacred history begins, for what comes before him in Genesis is sacred legend rather than history. It begins with an individual, a man who heard God's voice and obeyed; but an individual whose chief importance consists in his being the father of a chosen race. God's purpose begins to be revealed, that the many are to be saved by the few, who are called out of the mass in order that they may serve the many. With great skill the writer shows how many obstacles had to be overcome before even a start could be made in fulfilling this purpose. All the more wonderfully does Abraham's faith shine out.

This is the lesson of the Bible story. Its trimmings, as we might call them, are interesting but not important. By trimmings I mean the romantic descriptions of Abraham's early life found in reecnt books, based on the discoveries at Ur of the Chaldees. Abraham may have lived in one of the stately houses revealed by the spade; he and Sarah may have worn ornaments like those found in the ruins of Ur; he may have left the city as a protest against the worship of the Moon carried on there. But these are guesses, and the Bible is not interested in them. Most likely he was a desert sheikh who for a time lived in or near Ur and then migrated northwards to Haran, where the Bible places the start of his wanderings.

Was Abraham a tribe or an individual? A tribe certainly, for a man and his wife could not have taken these long journeys alone with safety. He had great flocks and herds and could muster an army of 318 men (Gen. 14. 14). But with equal certainty he was an individual. The tribe must have had a leader, who received the call and provided the inspiration for so many arduous journeys. So from the historian's point of view this was the beginning of a movement which after some 4,000 years resulted in the setting up of the modern State of Israel. But religiously it tells of the emergence of the first man in the world whom we know to have lived by faith in the promise of the unseen God, and by the vision of a far-off future for his descendants.

Abraham went to the south of Palestine and made Hebron his headquarters. For the Hebrew reader the buying of the case of Machpelah as a family grave was very important; the race of Abraham was staking out a claim to possess the whole land. Going down to Egypt was significant too; it fore-shadowed the years of Israel's sojourning in Egypt, their bitter experiences, and God's saving of his people from bondage. The story of Sodom and Gomorrah illustrates the choice between the pure faith of the desert and the corruption of city life, which was to confront Israel in centuries to come. The most beautiful of all the tales is that of Abraham's sacrificing Isaac. He was prepared to lose his beloved only son, the child of his old age, and with Isaac the hope that had sustained him in his wanderings, because it was God's will. Then came the voice from heaven telling him this was not the kind of sacrifice God wanted. In a wonderful way the story links the primitive ideas of a well meant but mistaken religion with the atoning death of Christ on the Cross.

One lesson we can learn from Abraham concerns his loneli-ness. The great pioneers in human history are those who, at least for a time, are prepared to go out into the wilderness and be alone. In the vast urban conglomerations of to-day, in which we all read the same newspapers, wear similar clothes, and listen to the same broadcasting of sound or picture, few people dare to break with convention and go out on a way of solitude, listening to God's voice. God still needs these lonely souls, who are never less alone than when alone, because their heavenly Father is with them, and they go out in the wilder-ness, hearing his voice and learning to be the men God means them to be.

6

Providence

God sent me before you . . . to save your lives by a great
deliverance. So now it was not you that sent me hither,
but God. GENESIS 45. 7, 8.

NOWHERE IN the Bible is there a better example of belief
in God's overruling providence than here, in the story of
Joseph. The tale begins with tragedy. The fine boy, his
father's favourite, is sold by his jealous brothers to be a slave
in Egypt. There he is unjustly accused by his master's wife
and thrown into prison. By a series of chance events, as they
might seem, which were really God's interventions, he reaches
the highest place in the kingdom, under Pharaoh. We need
not go into the historical background of all this. But it should
be said that there was one period in Egyptian history when
what seems unlikely was really quite possible. For some 150
years Egypt was ruled by foreign invaders, called Hyksos,
who came from Syria and Palestine. After they were expelled by a national uprising, and Egypt was free to develop
in its own way, the story of Joseph would be difficult to
believe, so great was the prejudice against foreigners. But
under a dynasty of Semitic rulers it would be natural for an
able young man from Palestine to reach high office.

The text comes from the beautiful passage in which Joseph
makes himself known to his brothers. They are smitten with
remorse, and recognize that no punishment would be too
severe for them. But Joseph is not only magnanimous; he lifts
the discussion onto a high and serene level. What they meant
as a petty revenge has been used by God as a means for
keeping his people alive in time of famine, that his purpose
for them may not be frustrated.

As we think over Joseph's words we realize their depth of

meaning. God chose the Hebrews to be his people, but his purpose could not have been fulfilled unless they had been educated for their destiny. The first step was to humble them by making them dwell for generations in a foreign land. The Bible passes over this period in silence; nothing happened worth recording. But, thanks to the accident of having a friend at Court, they were allowed to live in the land of Goshen, on the frontier, where they could preserve some at least of their national customs and not be absorbed by the Egyptians. The time came when their lot worsened and they were reduced to slavery. They were now "down and out", as we say. But "he that is down need fear no fall". Thanks to a great leader in Moses they were able to escape from Egypt and breathe the bracing air of the wilderness. The very fact that they escaped at all was a miracle, which enabled them to have a vivid sense of God's greatness and mercy. And so, with their minds fixed on the past and their eyes looking forward to the promised land, the history of the nation began.

Now what is history? Something more than one thing happening after another. The Greeks hardly got beyond that. Their two brilliant historians, Herodotus and Thucydides, never saw that history was the working out of God's purpose. And we, who are not historically minded people, generally live in the present. Whereas the Hebrews had their minds fixed on two points, one in the past the other in the future, and so discovered history. In the past was the great deliverance, "when Israel came out of Egypt". God who had done that for them had a further purpose in view. The future was at first the coming into Canaan and making it their own. When that was accomplished, the idea of the Kingdom of God gradually formed—an earthly kingdom of peace and righteousness of which the Lord was King, with a just and good prince of David's line as his representative. Israel then was unique in its belief in the sacredness of history, which was the working out of God's plan.

16

If we ask why the Hebrews alone developed like this, the answer is obvious. The other nations, like Egypt and Assyria, had a multitude of gods and goddesses, each trying to assert himself or herself, and so in practice neutralizing each other's effort. At first the Hebrews may not have been monotheists in the strict sense of the word, believing that their God existed and none other. But for them he was so vivid and forceful a person that he filled the picture and pushed the other gods aside. They were able to find a meaning in life just because they believed in a personal God, one with a will of his own which he would carry through inflexibly.

Another line they might have taken was to believe in Fate, an overruling destiny which was superior to any God or gods. That was a belief which was strongly held in later centuries and in the time of Christ was the working religion of many in the Roman Empire, showing itself in astrology, a kind of "science" that showed you your fate from the stars. How sad that many to-day go back to what St Paul called "the weak and beggarly elements" and believe that the masses of glowing gas that we call stars influence our lives!

Is not this belief in providence, the guiding hand of a just and merciful God, just what we need to recapture to-day, a personal God who cares for us and moulds our characters by the changes and chances of our lives? The life of each of us forms a pattern, which is the result of the influence of circumstances on the nature inherited from our parents. When we were young we set out to carve a career for ourselves. When we grow old we look back on the years and say with the hymn, "I loved to choose and see my path, but now lead thou me on". We are content to leave the final shaping of our lives to God. And, as we look back, we see how his providence has been guiding us all the while. Our failures and setbacks, which were desolating at the time, have been used to discipline our characters. No worse fate could have been ours than for all to go well. The Christian believes that this life is a school to train us for the life to come. If he is right, then we must own that life does its job amazingly well. If God grants us a quiet time of reflection before the end, we shall learn to say: "Except for my sins, I would not have had anything different."

7

"I am that I am"

I am that I am; *or better, as in the margin of the Revised Version:* I will be that I will be. EXODUS 3. 14.

MOSES HAS fled from Egypt and taken refuge with Jethro, the priest of Midian, in the wilderness, marrying his daughter. There as an exile he receives his call to lead Israel out of Egypt. And, the most important thing of all, he receives a revelation concerning the nature of God. The God whom his fathers served is with him still, but now for the first time he learns the true name of that God; and for the Hebrews the name meant personality and nature. Jacob at his birth received a name meaning "supplanter", the smooth tricky youth who knew how to look after himself; later he was given a new name, Israel, meaning something like "prince of God", to suit his changed character. So Simon in the Gospels is called Peter, "the Rockman", a name which itself gave him an ideal to live up to, which he did so splendidly.

Now this mysterious new name of God cannot mean "I am", for the simple reason that the Hebrew verb never means that. It must be translated "I will be (what I will be)". The new name revealed was Yahweh (in English traditionally called Jehovah), which is the same verb in the third person singular—"he will be (what he will be)". When God speaks, the word is put in the first person, naturally—"I will be". So, as naturally, when the Hebrews spoke of God, the third person was used—"he will be".[1]

This was one of the great moments in the history of religion, one to which all later thoughts of God can be traced back. Before we can realize its importance we must consider the ideas held about God at that time by other nations.

First let us think of national gods. On the far side of Jordan was the little country of Moab, whose god was Chĕmōsh. Chemosh was a personification of the people; if Moab was wiped out, Chemosh would cease to exist. From such a low estimate of its God Israel was preserved, as we shall see presently.

Now turn to Babylonia, in its way a very religious country, just as Egypt was. It had many gods. There was the sun-god, the moon-god, the great earth-mother, and the young god who represented the fresh vegetation of spring which dies down in the hot rainless months of summer, to rise again after rain—to mention only a few of the Babylonian divinities. All these were Nature-gods, personifying natural forces. They were confined to their own orbit and to what was always recurring. The sun rose every day, the moon had a cycle of twenty-eight days, the vegetation-god went through the process of dying and rising again each year. That is, they were personifications of Nature and in the last resort were not free agents; they had to do what Nature or Fate ordered them.

Israel's God was completely different. He was the living, acting God who did what he pleased. "I will be what I will be." So long as the world lasted he would be directing its course according to his will. "I will be what I will be." He did not obey Nature: Nature obeyed him.

[1] There are difficulties which cannot be gone into here, but this explanation is generally accepted.

Now notice exactly what was happening. The God whom Jethro and the Midianites ignorantly worshipped revealed himself to Moses: "I am the God your fathers worshipped, and my nature is far grander and fuller than anything they imagined. And I have chosen Israel to be my people, not for their merits, for they are an insignificant little nation, reduced to slavery, disobedient and backsliding, but as an act of free grace, of my mercy and condescension." This is the beginning of true spiritual religion, when man disowns his merits and humbly accepts God's gift. All this took place among a strange tribe, outside the borders of the Promised Land. And later, when God's will was revealed on Mount Sinai, again it was far away from the land of Israel. Long afterwards, when Elijah fled to be alone with God he went to Horeb (the other name for Sinai). All this was a wonderful help to Israel in the dark days to come: they knew that God was not confined to their own land but had been with them in Egypt and at the Red Sea, and on the mountain in Arabia. When they were tempted to think that because they had lost their land they had lost their God, the thought would recur: history teaches us that God chose us from outside, he is not tied down to any one place, and his greatest acts of power were performed outside our borders.

So Moses went back to his people with the great message that God, the living God, who had chosen them, was of a quality different from the gods of the Gentiles; he was absolutely self-determined, the living ruler of the world, who would be the unchanging background of their lives and yet would reveal different sides of his nature to meet their changing needs. Israel was slow in learning this lesson, but she always looked back to the Exodus as the real beginning, when God chose Israel as a child and called him out of Egypt. What the Resurrection is to the Christian the Exodus was to the Jews, the assurance that God was living and acting and saving, and would be their God for ever.

8

The Old Covenant

Behold the blood of the covenant, which the Lord hath made with you. EXODUS 24. 8.

THE IDEA of covenant is fundamental in the Bible, but we hardly realize this because in our English versions the word is sometimes translated "testament". The Old Testament is the book which tells us about God's Covenant with Israel and all that it implied: the New Testament is about the solemn pact or Covenant which God made with the Church. Both Covenants were made with blood, the first with the blood of animals, the second with that of Christ shed on the Cross.

In ordinary life we cannot dispense with agreements between man and man, and so it was in the ancient world. Long before any books were written, at a time when what we call literature existed only in the form of poems learned by heart and stories told by the camp fire, we find legal agreements, receipts for goods delivered, and so forth. Other things could be stored in the capacious memories of people who, having no artificial aids to memory, such as engagement books, could remember with ease; but business matters had to be recorded, for the two parties might remember differently. To avoid this, in solemn matters God was called in as a witness to the oaths taken, which no one then dared to repudiate, and a sacrifice was offered. When we read of the oath taken, "God do so to me and more also", often found in the Old Testament, we must imagine an animal being slain and a man declaring, "That be my fate if I fail to keep my word!" The most famous friendship in the Bible, that of David and Jonathan, was sealed by a covenant *before the Lord*, that is at an altar, with sacrifice (1 Sam. 23. 18). Two men took a pledge with God as witness, and it could not be broken. Another covenant is found in the story of the young king Josiah, who made a twofold covenant, with God and the people, to keep the Law of God (2 Kings 23. 3).

All that is by way of introduction, to lead up to the great covenant between God and Israel, with Moses representing God to Israel and Israel to God. The Law, and above all the Ten Commandments, has been given on Mount Sinai and is then read to the people, who accept it as their rule of life. Animals are sacrificed, and their blood is poured into basins. Moses then goes down the long rows of the people, sprinkling some blood on the altar, which represents God, and some on the people. It is the old custom of blood brotherhood, by which in a primitive tribe two men exchange blood and become brothers—but now it is applied to God and man. We to-day are squeamish and we are thankful to be spared such a messy performance; but no one then felt such scruples; it was a natural and impressive ceremony.

God and Israel are now one, joined by the closest of ties. He has chosen Israel and by the hand of Moses has led them out of Egypt. But this remains to be done, their solemn acceptance of the call and promise to do God's will. Ever afterwards the Hebrews looked back to this day—they were God's chosen people, what a glorious destiny! It was this feeling of election that has preserved the Jews down the centuries, during the bad times of exile and persecution; this, far more than any hope in the coming of the Messiah. Needless to say, they were often hard-hearted and stiff-necked, to use the Bible language, but prophets and teachers arose in each generation to recall them to their pledge and remind them of the Covenant. The point at issue between Jews and Christians is whether there has really been a new Covenant, effected by the blood of Christ, which has bound God and man together far more closely than was ever possible under the old Covenant. St Paul says that a blindness has fallen on

22

the eyes of the Jews, so that the glory of the offer of salvation is veiled from them (2 Cor. 3. 14).

There are two parties to this pact at Mount Sinai, man and God. Man is bound by the pledge taken by the fathers in the wilderness and continually renewed in the years that followed. How about God? And here comes in the depth and beauty of the Old Testament religion. You cannot bind God. *But you can trust him.* And so we get salvation by faith here at the beginning of the Bible. Men trust in his loving kindness, his loyalty to the pledge. He has given his word and will not go back on it. In the last resort the Hebrew belief rested on the nature of God. It was a superb act of faith, which in spite of continual back-slidings was repeated continually by the best spirits of the nation down the ages until the present day. Whatever prejudices we may have felt against particular Jews, let us judge Judaism by its noble spirits, who have been very noble indeed.

9

Sacrifices

I beseech you therefore, brethren . . . that ye present your bodies a living sacrifice, holy, acceptable to God.

ROMANS 12. 1.

THESE WORDS sweep away a venerable institution, deep rooted in the past history of religion, and put something in the place of sacrifice, something simple and beautiful but very hard to make real. Which of us can be sure that he does offer his whole self, his body and soul to God, as in the service of Holy Communion we say we do?

The sacrifices of the Old Testament are difficult to understand. One problem is the attitude of the great prophets, especially Amos and Jeremiah, towards them. They say quite definitely that in the wilderness period God did not order sacrifices (Jer. 7. 22, compare Amos 5. 25), which seems to contradict the plain words of the Bible elsewhere. Perhaps the best explanation is that all the nations of the East at that time offered sacrifices, which therefore had nothing specially Hebrew about them. The Bible begins with Cain and Abel offering the fruits of the earth and a lamb respectively. There is nothing to explain why they did this. Sacrifice was probably on a very small scale in the wilderness, and the Law of Moses regulated what little was done; the Hebrews followed the practice of the nations round them, and the great religious ideas of the Old Testament had little to do with sacrifice.

The different kinds of sacrifice—peace-offerings, whole burnt-offerings, sin-offerings, guilt-offerings, freewill offerings, thank-offerings, and first fruits—are puzzling and indeed are not worth trying to remember. Let us try to simplify the subject.

There were two main kinds of sacrifice: the peace-offering and all the rest. The peace-offering began in this way. In the early days of the Hebrews in Canaan meat was rarely eaten. Suppose a farmer had a lamb that he could spare. He would kill the animal and prepare it for a meal. In that hot climate it would not keep long, so he would invite neighbours to share it with himself and family. The feast was a religious ceremony, and probably at this period all meat was eaten in this way. The father in a sense was the priest of his family (anyhow he did the sacrificing), but the local priest would be invited to see that all was done properly and would get a little meat for his trouble. The blood was poured on a simple altar of earth and soon disappeared, showing that it had gone to God. And the smoke of the roasted animal was seen to dissolve in the air and go to God. The whole atmosphere was one of peace, with both God and man. This has a bearing on our religion to-day, for the Passover, out of which the

24

Eucharist grew, was a peace-offering festival. There is no need to worry about the details of the other sacrifices in order to understand the meaning of the Eucharist. As St Paul says, "Christ our Passover is sacrificed for us; therefore let us keep the feast". Holy Communion is first and foremost a time of peace and joy.

The other animal sacrifices had a different origin. The victim was wholly destroyed, except for a small part, such as the skin, which went to the priest. The idea was a gift to God, the great King, either tribute such as an earthly king expected or a freewill offering. The purpose was to win God's favour and especially to atone for sin. The twice daily sacrifice of a lamb in the Temple was especially to atone for national sins. To do justice to the Jews, they did not dream of extorting salvation from God, indeed, more and more, as time went on, they laid stress on the repentance and prayers which accompanied sacrifices, and really bad sins, what the Bible calls "sinning with a high hand", were not covered by sacrifice. But they did try to deserve salvation by these gifts and other good works. And, in gratitude for recovery from sickness or other mercies, it was natural to offer an animal.

The story of sacrifice is to our minds pathetic. Multitudes of men destroyed animals which might have provided meals for themselves and their families. The idea which naturally occurs to us, "Why this waste of good food?" is not hinted at in the Bible. So strongly entrenched were the old ideas that the words of the prophets and psalmists declaring the useless-ness of sacrifice were not taken seriously.

We get some idea of the power of the Cross when we see how all this burden, which had lasted thousands of years, was lifted from the shoulders of the first Christians, when they realized that they could never deserve salvation but must accept it as the free gift of God. In place of the Jewish sacri-fices the Church put the spiritual sacrifice of ourselves, our souls and bodies, offered to God in union with the perfect

25

sacrifice and obedience of Christ. That is much harder to do properly; we are not let off easily, and so long as we live we shall bewail our imperfect response to God's love. But we cannot go back. Sacrifice of animals played a valuable part in the early days of man's development. Now, as Abraham said to Isaac, "God will provide himself a lamb"—the Lamb of God who by his self-offering took away the sins of the world.

10

The Day of Atonement

The high priest entereth into the holy place year by year.
HEBREWS 9. 25.

THE HEBREW year began about the end of September; after the return from exile the date was moved six months earlier, though the old date continued to be observed as a sort of "ecclesiastical" New Year. It was a great time for the people of Israel. Besides the actual start of the year there was the feast of Tabernacles, which rounded off the agricultural festivals. And on the tenth day of the first month the most striking of all the Hebrew observances took place, the Day of Atonement. This is described in one chapter, Leviticus 16, and not mentioned elsewhere in the Old Testament. The chapter comes in a late source, but the service is so primitive in character that it must be very early. It was the only regular fast day ("ye shall afflict your souls") and had to be observed as if it was also a Sabbath.

The high priest on this day only went behind the veil and entered the Holy of Holies. He first made atonement for himself by a sacrifice. Then two goats were brought to him, on which he cast lots: one was for the Lord, the other for

Azazel. The Hebrew word denotes a demon of the wilderness, but the Authorized Version, making a shot at the meaning, translates "scapegoat"; this must be wrong, for the animal did not escape death. The first goat was killed, and the high priest sprinkled its blood on the mercy-seat and made atonement for the holy place and the altar and for the sins of Israel. This is remarkable. The Hebrews acknowledge that the whole sacrificial system is contaminated with sin and needs to be purified. Even more remarkable is the next step. He lays his hands on the live goat and confesses the sins of Israel, which in an acted parable he transfers to the animal. A man is in waiting to lead the goat into the wilderness. According to later tradition it was killed by being thrown over a precipice. Perhaps in early days it was left to be devoured by wild beasts. In any case it did not return, and the transaction symbolized the removal of sin from Israel. How far this was taken literally we do not know. We might well quote the psalm: "It cost more to redeem their soul, so that he must leave that alone for ever."

The picture of national penitence is most impressive. This was something different from the ordinary run of sacrifices. On this day of the year alone the dark inner chamber of the Holy of Holies, which represented the presence of God, was entered—by the high priest alone, and then only after all these precautions.

For Christians the ritual is important because of its application to Christ in the New Testament. Christ is depicted as Son of God, Son of Man, Messiah, Son of David, Prophet, and so on. But except in the Epistle to the Hebrews (see chapter 9) he is not described as Priest. There he appears as the second and greater Aaron and High Priest, making atonement for the sins of his people. But what a difference between the two figures! We, who have to look up the passage in Leviticus in order to follow the argument, find it impressive. To those familiar with the Law of Moses from childhood it must have been magnificent. Compare the two pictures, says the writer. The Jewish High Priest—and Christ. A ceremony that had to be repeated every year—and the once for all and final act of redemption. An earthly priest entering the inmost chamber of the Temple—and our Saviour ascending into heaven. And lastly, a man offering the blood of a goat—and the Son of God offering his own blood and precious life to God on our behalf.

Christ is the Redeemer of mankind. His life is in heaven, where he continually lives to intercede for us. Our ideas of the Ascension are largely based on the Epistle to the Hebrews, which in its turn goes back to the old Jewish service of the Day of Atonement.

11

Prophets and Priests

Would God that all the Lord's people were prophets.
NUMBERS 11. 29.

THE BOOK of Numbers has a curious story. Seventy men, seized by a divine impulse, prophesy. Probably we must imagine something like what St Paul had to deal with at Corinth, an outburst of prayer and praise, often in unintelligible words, which comes suddenly and goes as suddenly. Anyhow, in this case the outburst dies down; we are told "they did so no more"—except for two men, Eldad and Modad, about whom Moses receives a complaint. They may have seemed to be presuming and claiming a position which only Moses, who is acknowledged to be *the* prophet, might hold. But Moses is magnanimous and merely says, "Would God that all the Lord's people were prophets".

This happened at a time when Moses was laying the foundations of the Laws, in which priests played a great part. He himself belonged to the priestly tribe of Levi, and his brother Aaron was the head of the priests. Yet he said in effect: "We want both, priests *and* prophets. We of the priestly tribe welcome all the help we can get from other men who are called by God." Let us then consider the problem: "Priests or prophets?" to which the answer surely is: "Priests *and* prophets".

The priest is the permanent man, on whom the institutions of the Church depend. He is the minister and steward of the Word and Sacraments; he is the officer, who leads the people in sacred things; and he is the pastor, who can never get away from his responsibilities. In the Old Testament he offers sacrifice; in the New Testament he sets the example of offering spiritual sacrifices of ourselves, our souls and bodies.

In the Acts of the Apostles we find first the Apostles, appointed by Christ; then the deacons, chosen from (apparently) the younger men, to relieve the Apostles of the burden of administration; then a council of presbyters or elders. But there were also prophets, raised up by God and obviously filled with the Spirit of God. If they were inspired by God, and if the regular ministers of the Church were sometimes dull dogs (as they are of necessity in every generation—we can't all be gifted), why did they not take the first place of authority?

First, it belongs to the nature of prophecy that it cannot be relied on. As our text says, "they did so no more". The prophet is inspired and able to inspire others. But he has to be "in form" as we say. His powers come and go, and in any case are liable to die down as he grows old. You can't depend on him as you can on the right kind of priest.

Secondly, the prophet has a habit of seeing one thing at a time. He proclaims some neglected truth, very important no doubt, but when repeated continually, liable to become monotonous. So no doubt do the sermons of ordained priests sometimes, but they at least try to keep in mind the whole of revealed truth.

Thirdly, the prophet generally has a keen eye for abuses, which he denounces unsparingly. Such reformers are necessary, as we see from the prophets of the Old Testament. But even they, inspired as they were, tend to bore us by their constant repetitions. There is so much "Woe, woe", and so little "Comfort ye my people".

Let us look at some prophets in fairly recent times. The outstanding example is George Fox, founder of the Society of Friends, generally called Quakers. He is generally associated with non-resistance and absolute pacifism, which are derived from texts in the Sermon on the Mount. Individuals can put them into practice, but for a State to adopt them would be disastrous; a criminal would always "get away with it". But his real doctrine was the Inner Light, God within the soul, which he held so strongly that he abolished Creeds and Sacraments and forms of prayers. This is a good example of a prophet who calls attention to one truth at the cost of neglecting others.

William Booth also deserves mention. To begin with a Methodist, he founded his own Society, the Salvation Army, and went out among the poor and degraded folk of Victorian England, preaching the gospel of salvation and caring for bodies as well as souls. But his prophetic gifts were not sufficient to carry on the work, and he had to rely on an institution, a kind of Church with rigid military discipline, which has been compared to the Society of Jesuits. Everyone had to obey him; a prophet himself, he did not tolerate any other man rising up and challenging his authority.

Our Lord warned us that there would be false prophets. We cannot regard Mrs Eddy, the founder of Christian Science, as anything but one of these. For her, matter does not exist: sin, pain, illness, and death are illusions. The gateway to release is prayer, which means realizing that they are non-existent. The contrast with the Gospel story, in which the Son of God takes flesh and suffers and dies, in reality not by illusion, is glaring, and no reconciliation between historic Christianity and Christian Science is possible.

12

Samson and Jesus

What manner of child shall this be?
LUKE 1, 66.

NONE OF us can make much of the book of Judges, least of all if we sample it for devotional reading. It depicts the rough and tumble of a primitive age, and people behave— well, very much as they do sometimes in our own parishes. But it is good to be reminded how stony was the soil out of which grew the flowers of Hebrew spirituality. However, amid the fighting and bloodshed we find one chapter of rare beauty, shining with the light of an old Italian picture. I refer to the thirteenth chapter, which tells of the birth of Samson.

Manoah, a pious rustic, and his wife have been denied the blessing of children. One day the angel of the Lord appears to the wife in the form of a prophet and gives her the promise, "Thou shalt conceive and bear a son". She is to drink no wine, and the son is to be a Nazarite, that is, drink no wine and use no razor. Alarmed by the messenger, she hastens to tell her husband. He prays to the Lord that the messenger may come again and give fuller instruction. Later the angel returns, and the woman fetches her husband, to whom this time the message is given: the wife must be very pure and

31

worthy of her vocation. The angel refuses to eat with them but bids them offer sacrifice. This they do, and he disappears in the flame of the sacrifice and goes back to heaven. Manoah is alarmed: we have seen God and must die. But his wife has more faith: if God had meant to kill us, he would not have accepted the sacrifice.

This sounds familiar—where have we heard something like this before? Why, of course, in the first chapter of St Luke, in the story of the Annunciation. The angel Gabriel comes to Mary and says, "thou shalt conceive and bring forth a son". She too is alarmed but humbly accepts God's will for her. There is nothing about the child's being brought up as a Nazarite, but something like it is told of the child promised by an angel to Elizabeth her cousin, the child who was to be known as John the Baptist; he also was to abstain from strong drink. The message of the angel to Manoah is represented by the words spoken to Joseph in a dream, as told by St Matthew. Both the language and the inner spirit of the Old and New Testament stories are alike. The fact is, St Luke knew his Bible well and naturally wrote in the same way as the book of Judges.

So the two lives, of Samson and Jesus, began alike. The two boys lay in their cradles and except to the fond eyes of the mother each must have looked very like other babies. Each mother must have cherished the same hope, that her boy would grow up to be a Saviour for Israel. But how did the lives continue?

Samson became the village hero of those rough times. A man of prodigious strength and broad humour, unprincipled in his dealings with women, the natural leader of young men, he won great renown and is described as a Judge of Israel. Now the Judge at this period of Old Testament history was a military leader who saved Israel from her enemies, and "Saviour" gives the meaning best. Samson performs wonders of valour. On one occasion he was filled with the spirit and seized a young lion, tearing it in pieces (Judges 14. 6); and again, when he was tightly bound with cords, "the Spirit of the Lord came mightily upon him" and he rent them asunder like flax (15. 14). The end of the story is famous. Samson is captured by the Philistines, thanks to the cunning of Delilah; his eyes are put out, and "eyeless in Gaza" he is kept in prison and made to grind corn. Then they bring him out to make sport for three thousand people crowded on the roof of a great house, as a kind of grandstand. He grasps the two centre pillars and brings them down, involving himself and the spectators in the ruins. "So the dead which he slew at his death were more than they which he slew in his life" (16. 30).

Now turn to the other baby and see what manner of man he became. He too was a Saviour, but one who came to save men's lives, not to destroy them. As for enemies, his teaching was "love your enemies", and as an example of unselfish kindness he chose a Samaritan, not a Jew. He too was filled with the Spirit, but that was the Holy Spirit of God, which drove him into the wilderness to contend with evil and defeat it by spiritual means alone. In the final act of the drama he too was killed, his heart all the time filled with love for his persecutors, his lips saying, "Father, forgive them, for they know not what they do".

It is difficult not to be sentimental over a newborn baby, but we must ask the question, What manner of child shall this be? He may become a saint of God, or a criminal, or even a scourge of the human race. If they are Christians, his parents surround him with prayers, but they are realists and know that he is born into a sinful world and may turn out badly. So they lose no time in bringing him into the fellowship of the Church by Holy Baptism. They recall Christ's wards, "of such is the kingdom of God", and they never cease to pray that the rest of his life may be worthy of this beginning.

13

The Hebrew King

Nay; but a king shall reign over us: when the Lord your
God was your king. 1 Samuel 12. 12.

THE FASCINATING story of the choice of the king of Israel
is told in the book of Samuel. Fascinating, because of the
vivid description of two opposite points of view. First we are
told that a king was a good thing and God's gift to Israel.
Then that to ask for a king was an act of disloyalty towards
God, who alone was Israel's king. Which view was right?

The Bible never minds putting opposing views before us.
We might write an essay, giving the pros and cons and then
summing up in our own words. But the writer of Samuel
gives two stories, one for and the other against, and leaves
his readers to reconcile them. They will agree that kingship,
like other human institutions, was both bad and good; at
the moment it was necessary, but it contained the seeds of
evil, and the writer looking back on the tangled history saw
more clearly than was possible at the time what the Hebrews
were letting themselves in for.

The state of things could not have been worse. The twelve
tribes were something like the Highland clans of old Scotland
—bound together by ties of race and religion but each going
its own way and unable to unite against the common enemy.
As a result the Hebrews had been conquered by the Philistines
and had been so disarmed that they had nothing with which
to sharpen their farm instruments except files for small tools
and had to go to the Philistines to have the others sharpened.
So Samuel was told by God to anoint Saul to be a military
leader ("captain" is the word used), who by his military
skill would unite the tribes and lead them against their
enemies. It was all perfectly natural, and Saul fulfilled the

hopes set on him and for a time won a measure of independence. The difficulty arose when the question was asked, What do you mean by a king? The representatives of Israel asked for a king, to be "like all the nations" round about. The best known of those nations were Egypt and Babylon, where the king was looked on as divine. The Hebrews never had a king like that. Even David, whose name was to be so renowned, had to be *made king* first by Judah (2 Sam. 2. 4.), then by the northern tribes (5. 3). In each case we are told that "they anointed him king", suggesting a constitutional monarchy, based on the will of the people. When Solomon died, his son Rehoboam went to Shechem to meet the tribes; they did not, as we should expect, come to him. Bargaining took place and, Rehoboam's answers being unsatisfactory, the northern tribes broke away and set up their own king, Jeroboam. Nearly three hundred years later the young king Josiah made a covenant with God in front of the people, which they accepted. He could not bind them without their consent.

Then how do we explain the expressions in the Psalms which suggest that the king was at least half-divine; for example, "Thou art my Son; this day have I begotten thee" (Psalm 2. 7)? The Psalm, which was a hymn sung at the Coronation of a king, represents God as *adopting* the new king, who becomes God's son. But Israel was already God's son, as we learn from God's words to Moses in the wilderness, "Thus saith the Lord, Israel is my son" (Ex. 4. 22), and from the message to Hosea, "When Israel was a child, then I loved him and called my son out of Egypt" (Hos. 11. 1). The king was God's son in that he represented the people, who were already his son, to God.

We are justified then when we see in constitutional monarchy an institution approved by God in the Old Testament. Ideally, there Church and State are two aspects of the same thing. But in the New Testament there is a very different state of things. The Jews formed a province of the vast Roman Empire, being governed either by a Roman official or by a vassal king like Herod. They for the most part had a passionate hate of their overlords, which led to the frightful war that began in A.D. 66 and lasted till 70, when Jerusalem fell and the Temple was destroyed. When Jesus began his ministry Tiberius was Emperor of Rome (Luke 3. 1) and he was still on the throne when Jesus said, "Render unto Caesar the things that are Caesar's". And when St Paul said, "The powers that be are ordained of God" (Rom. 13. 1), Nero was Emperor. If historians to-day think that Tiberius was not so bad as he has been painted, no one white-washes Nero. The Church began as a tiny minority in a vast heathen State, to which it was loyal.

The people of Britain and the Dominions have a Christian monarchy a thousand years old, dating back to King Alfred. Such an example of stability in a changing world is enormously impressive, quite apart from the personal character of recent sovereigns, which has reinforced the prestige of the Crown so greatly. It would be the duty of Christians to make the best of a pagan State, as the early Christians did in their time. But when the Sovereign, besides being the power ordained by God, is a practising Christian, dedicated to God's service in the wonderful service of the Coronation, our duty of obedience to the Throne is reinforced by passionate loyalty.

14

The Young Man David

His (Solomon's) heart was not perfect with the Lord his God,
as was the heart of David his father. 1 KINGS 11. 4.

WHEN WE read the story of David, with its mixture of
nobility and meanness, we find it hard to endorse the Bible
verdict, that his heart was perfect with God. The best defence
we can make, remembering that for the Hebrews "heart"
meant primarily "will", is to say that he tried up to the limit
of his ability to serve God, but that when he grew older and
had almost absolute power the temptations of his high
position proved too strong for him. When he died, the
Hebrews summing up his whole life agreed that its general
tendency was good, and that it had conferred so many blessings on Israel that he must be regarded as a good king. Even
so, "perfect" is a strong word, and they must have forgotten
his worse side. Let us think to-day of the chivalrous youth
who won the hearts of his followers, leaving for another time
his later years, when the clouds came up and obscured the
bright morning sky.

The story begins with the boy as he tends his father's sheep
and faces dangers from wild beasts. He told Saul that he had
confronted a lion, which he took by the beard and killed. Was
this just a boy's boast? Hardly, in view of his other martial
exploits, such as the fight with Goliath. This intrepid youth
was summoned home to meet the awe-inspiring Samuel (1
Sam. 16. 4) and be anointed as king in place of Saul. Next
we read of his adventures at the Court of Saul, who was
afflicted by periodical fits of madness, in which he tried to
kill his page.

But there are better things than these. First we note his
chivalry, when he had the chance of killing Saul, who was

asleep with his guards. That was a short way to safety and success, which he refused to take. David's followers cherished an enthusiastic devotion for their noble leader, as is seen from the charming story of his thirst. One day, when he was in his remote fortress, he exclaimed, "Oh that one would give me water to drink from the well of Bethlehem, which is by the gate!" Three of his men heard it and went off, no doubt by night, evaded the sentinels of the Philistines who were then occupying Bethlehem, drew the water, and brought it to David. He refused to drink, but poured it out as a drink-offering to the Lord, saying, "Shall I drink of the blood of the men who went in jeopardy of their lives?" (1 Sam. 23).

Even more remarkable than his chivalry was his love for Jonathan, Saul's son. The two young men were rivals for power and might have been deadly enemies. But no, at first sight Jonathan "loved him as his own soul" (2 Sam. 18. 3). He pleaded with his father for David's life. The story of their farewell is exquisitely told, and the friendship is always regarded as the perfect example of a man's pure and un-selfish friendship for another man; though as it stands in the Bible it reflects more glory on Jonathan than on David. David's lament over Jonathan, killed by the Philistines in battle, is touchingly beautiful.

> I am distressed for thee, my brother Jonathan:
> Very pleasant hast thou been unto me:
> Thy love for me was wonderful,
> Passing the love of women.

(2 Sam. 1. 26)

With this attractive side of David went other tendencies which were to develop in later years. No one can live as a leader of a band of insurgents without exercising cunning as well as skill. Obviously David at one stage lived largely by blackmail, levying dues on farmers in return for protection, which meant not pillaging them. He had to play a double game with the Philistines, to whom he had fled from Saul, pretending to help them but really working against their interests. "All is fair in war", runs the motto, but unless a man is very careful the habits formed in war will persist in peace and lead to deterioration of character, especially if he is in a position of power. Next time we shall trace the steps of this deterioration in David.

15

The Old Man David

Would God I had died for thee, O Absalom, my son, my son. 2 SAMUEL 18. 33.

WE LEFT David in his stronghold in the south of Judah, playing a double game with the Philistines, eluding Saul's attempts to catch him, levying toll on farmers to support his troops, and gaining the enthusiastic devotion of his men. Then came the death of Saul and his three sons in battle with the Philistines. What was left of the Israelite army retreated beyond Jordan, and the Philistines became masters of the land.

The sequel was astounding. In a few years David beat the Philistines, won over the northern tribes, established a capital in the newly conquered city of Jerusalem (skilfully put on neutral ground to avoid antagonizing either North or South), and extended his rule over the border countries up to Damascus and beyond. It was a miracle of vigour and skilful statesmanship. Ascribed at the time to the favour of God, it had of course its human side. Neither Egypt nor Assyria was then strong and active, and the new empire could arise without opposition.

In 2 Samuel chapters 9 to 20, we have a detailed account of the later years of David, written in a racy and impressive manner, evidently by some man who had lived at the Court and taken part in the events described. The main purpose is to show how the way was made open for Solomon to ascend the throne. To us the interest lies in the growing weakness of David, caused by his unhappy family life. He had many wives, though nothing like the number credited to Solomon. If the Old Testament seems to allow polygamy, it at least lets us see what a dance the king's wives led their husband. Polygamy brings its own punishment in the quarrels of the wives and their respective children; David was quite unable to control his sons.

In the famous story of Uriah the Hittite David bids Joab put Uriah in the forefront of the battle, where he was sure to be killed, in order that he might take Bathsheba, Uriah's beautiful wife. When David dismisses the death of the brave soldier as one of the inevitable incidents of war, we are disgusted. We realize the truth of Lord Acton's famous saying, "All power tends to corrupt, and absolute power corrupts absolutely". Against the background of the ancient East what follows is startling. Nathan the prophet comes and denounces David for his meanness. The king accepts the rebuke and repents. Imagine, if you can, this happening in Assyria. A prophet, if there had been one there, would have been instantly killed for such behaviour to royalty.

The sad but fascinating story of Absalom forms the climax of David's reign. On the one hand a clever and attractive young man felt that the old king was in his dotage and that he could make a better job of ruling the country. On the other hand David had made a half-hearted attempt to control his son, but, torn between his duty as king and his love for Absalom, he had never pursued a policy for long. When Absalom set up his standard of rebellion, David lost his nerve and fled from Jerusalem. It is pathetic to read of the devotion shown to their old foe by the mercenary soldiers of Philistine extraction, and by the best of his old friends. At this moment of his broken fortunes David made an utterance which is a landmark in the history of religion. When his followers brought the Ark with all its sacred associations out of Jerusalem he said, Send it back; if the Lord wants to save us, he can do it without the Ark. He would not have the holy chest treated as a mascot. The reader's disappointment at the king's crumpling up in the face of disaster is outweighed by pity when he comes to the battle. Absalom is killed, and David is overwhelmed with grief (victory at this price is not worth having). The old feud between North and South flares up again when David favours Judah which has rebelled against him rather than the tribes of the North which have backed him. The return to Jerusalem is an anti-climax, a disappointment to everyone rather than a triumph.

The pathos deepens when David's end is recounted. Adonijah seizes the kingdom. He was the eldest son and marked out to succeed. Why should he not anticipate things a little and take power into his vigorous hands? Nobody could respect a king who could not keep warm and had to get a young woman to cherish him. By a palace intrigue Solomon is proclaimed king, just in time to make Adonijah's followers melt away. Then comes the death-bed scene, when David pays off old scores by telling Solomon to get rid of Joab, his loyal old supporter. No life story in the Bible is told so fully and impartially. Remembering the heroic early days and the temptations of an absolute monarch, perhaps after all, viewing the life as a whole, we shall conclude that David was a good king.

Anyhow, this was how later generations judged David, whom they exalted to a pinnacle of heroism and even sanctity. But how splendidly frank the Bible is! The story is told fully, and nothing is hushed up, so that we can form our own conclusions.

16

Elijah on Mount Carmel

If the Lord be God, follow him: but if Baal, then follow him. 1 KINGS 18. 21.

THE STORY of Elijah on Mount Carmel is one of a people's decision when faced with two alternative policies. Such decisions are constantly being made in history; nearly always the popular emotion is focused in the will and driving power of one man, who knows what he wants and gets it. So it was here.

Elijah came from Gilead beyond Jordan, where he was a "sojourner", and we may suppose that his original home was the desert, which was comparatively untouched by the degradation of religion in central Israel. The name means "Jah (Yahweh) is my God", and his father must have given it to his baby as a confession of faith; the name would be an inspiration to the boy as he grew up. Anyhow, in the Bible he appears suddenly, without introduction, and throws himself into the religious struggle of his time. His great enemy was a woman, Ahab's wife Jezebel, who had made Baal-worship the established religion of the kingdom.

The issue at stake needs explanation. The word *baal* means "lord" and was carelessly used of the God of Israel, whose personal name was Yahweh (in the English Bible sometimes taking the form of Jehovah but more often spelled in capital letters as "the LORD"). A good illustration is Saul's giving his son the name Ishbaal, "man of Baal". Saul was a devout worshipper of the Hebrew God and must have meant "man of Yahweh". Later, the scribes who copied the Bible shrank from writing the accursed name of Baal and instead wrote Ishbosheth, "man of shame", Baal being a shame to Israel. They did this only in the books of Samuel, the old form

Ishbaal remaining in Chronicles. Now the confusion of Yahweh and Baal, dangerous as it was, need not have done permanent damage to Hebrew religion. But with Jezebel a new element had come in. She was daughter of the king of Tyre, in whose dominion Baal was worshipped as God of heaven, a universal god who excluded all rivals. Her aim therefore was to drive out Israel's God and substitute the worship of her own god. We must suppose her to have been sincere by her lights and to have carried king Ahab with her.

When Ahab heard that Elijah was organizing a resistance movement, as we might call it, he contrived a meeting, at which he accepted Elijah's proposal to arrange a trial of strength between the rival gods, to show which was the stronger. The ancient sanctuary of Carmel was chosen as the battleground. We know the story so well. The sacrifice is prepared, and the prophets of Baal have the first innings. From morning till three in the afternoon they dance round the altar and invoke their god—nothing happens. Elijah mocks. A fine sort of God! You must make more noise and wake him up; or perhaps he is not at home to-day. Then Elijah's turn comes: he prays and God hears; lightning descends from heaven and burns up the sacrifice. There is a tremendous revulsion of opinion; the people obey Elijah's commands and slaughter the prophets of Baal.

The splendid story has its difficulties. To begin with, there is the miracle, which seems to be what is called a miracle of coincidence, a natural event happening at the opportune moment. Just as in the story of Exodus, where a strong east wind drove back the shallow waters of the lake, so it was here. Fire from heaven does come sometimes and do great damage. On this occasion it came just when it was needed to save God's people from final apostasy. The way was prepared by the events of the previous three years, which had witnessed a disastrous drought. The Hebrews were ready to acknowledge that the drought was a punishment for deserting their

God and, perhaps reflecting that when there was lightning a break-up of the weather might be expected, experienced a violent revulsion of mood. This revulsion was expressed in a massacre of the prophets of Baal, undertaken by Elijah's orders. This rather shocks us, but even in our own days such things are done. Perhaps in the body of the State surgical operations are necessary at times. We have only to look at English history in the Tudor period, when executions were very frequent, to realize that our own people have not very long outgrown such violent methods; lamentable as they were, they at least saved England from the horrors of civil war which devastated France and Germany at that time.

For the final verdict on Elijah, his devotion and driving power and violence, we turn to the Gospels. Jesus said that no greater man than John the Baptist had arisen (Matt. 11. 11), and that John was Elijah come to life again (Matt. 11. 14), meaning that John and Elijah were both the agents of a great work of national repentance. As for Elijah's methods, once James and John wanted to call fire down from heaven on a village that would not receive their Master, as Elijah had done on his opponents, but Jesus said, "Ye know what spirit ye are of" (Luke 9. 55).

17

Elijah on Mount Horeb

What doest thou here, Elijah? 1 KINGS 19. 9.

THE PREVIOUS chapter tells of Elijah's victory over Baal-worship on Mount Carmel, so it is a surprise to read of his flight to Mount Horeb, far away from the land of Israel. We should deduce from this that, as often happens after a revolution, a strong reaction has set in; Jezebel is hitting back. But perhaps the Bible writer has put two stories together without troubling about the precise order and this really happened before the scene on Carmel.

To-day's story is one of the most dramatic in the Bible. Jezebel, infuriated by the massacre of her priests, threatens to arrest and kill Elijah, who escapes to the far south. His stupendous victory has turned into failure. "I am not better than my fathers", he cries; neither I nor they could stand up against such odds. Encouraged by an angel, he goes on his journey until he reaches the holy mountain of Horeb, another name for Sinai.

His motive is obvious. Where better could he go to get strength than to the scene of God's revelation to Moses, of the making of the Covenant between God and Israel, and of the giving of the Law? Here surely he will meet God and be rewarded for his toilsome pilgrimage. But no! The divine voice says, "What dost thou here, Elijah?" Your place is not here, in safety, but in the forefront of the battle for God against his enemies, in the land of Israel with all its dangers. God revealed himself on Carmel as the God of power, sending fire from heaven. Now he shows himself in another light, not in the thunder and lightning of the old story of Exodus, but in gentleness and quiet. First comes a hurricane, but God is not in that; then an earthquake; then a fire (lightning no doubt is meant). But God is not in these. Then comes "a still small voice", bringing the authentic message of the Almighty. What does it say? Go back to the firing-line, play your part in the stormy history of the northern kingdom; and, the climax, anoint Elisha to be your successor. Take long views, prepare for the future; the good work will go on after you are dead. Again, you are wrong when you say, "I, even I only, am left". There is a solid core of 7,000 faithful people who are loyal to the faith of their fathers.

There are two lessons to be learned from the story.

First, the manner of revelation. John Keble in his Whitsun-
tide hymn exactly expresses the teaching of the Bible.

> When God of old came down from heaven
> In power and wrath he came;
> Before his feet the clouds were riven,
> Half darkness and half flame.

This describes Sinai. But in the New Testament Pentecost
takes the place of Sinai.

> But when he came a second time
> He came in power and love;
> Softer than gale at morning prime
> Hovered his holy Dove.

Elijah's experience on Horeb prefigured the descent of the
Holy Ghost on the day of Pentecost. God has a new way of
teaching, suited to the needs of his people as they grow up
and become mature. This is the New Testament in the Old.

Secondly, the message which Elijah received is one that
applies to all of us. The more tender-hearted we are, the more
at times we long to get out of the turmoil of our present life.
We cry, "O that I had wings like a dove: for them would I
flee away and be at rest". God's answer is No. "There is no
discharge in that war" (Eccles. 8. 8), you have to keep on
struggling all your life. The hurly-burly of the daily struggle
may be distasteful, but we must go back to it and play our
part manfully. Our chief duty is to hand on the faith to the
next generation. Our example goes for much, but happy are
we if we can be active teachers, planting the faith in the hearts
of the young, so that they in their turn may testify as we have
done. "Anoint Elisha to be prophet in thy place."

Finally, we must never despair. We may think that we are
fighting the battle alone, but there are 7,000 in Israel who
are fighting with us. However difficult in some places it may
be to find them, we must cherish the belief that the Lord has

many people in our parish, secret believers perhaps but in their hearts on our side.

18

A Great Woman

I dwell among mine own people. 2 KINGS 4. 13.

LET US think to-day of the most charming of the stories told about Elisha. It concerns a "great" lady living at Shunem, great no doubt because of the position of her husband. As Elisha was passing one day she insisted on giving him a meal. This became a regular practice whenever he went that way. But she wanted to do more for this "holy man of God", as she called him. So she consulted her husband. Like other people in a good position, they lived in a house with a substantial flat roof approached by an outside staircase. Why not wall off part of it to make a spare bedroom? It would not need much furniture; a bed, table, chair, and lamp would be enough for the simple needs of the prophet. Then we can put it at his disposal, to come and go whenever he likes. Of course we shall go on feeding him as before.

All went according to plan. It is a good example of the proverbial Eastern hospitality. It was good manners to accept the offer, but good manners also dictated that hospitality should in some form be returned. That was impossible for a wandering prophet. So Elisha made a suggestion. Shall I put in a word for you with the king? This probably means, would you like your husband to go and live at Samaria and be one of the king's friends? I expect I can manage it for you. The lady answered bravely, "I dwell among mine own people". I am happy here, where everyone knows me. The clan will look after us if any misfortune comes our way. We certainly don't want to be mixed up with the Court and its intrigues. Women are much the same in all ages, and perhaps she also thought, "I have not proper clothes". How can we help her then? asks Elisha of Gehazi his servant, who says the one thing she wants is a son, for she is childless. Elisha boldly promises that she will be a happy mother by this time next year. "Nay, my lord, thou man of God, do not lie unto thine handmaid", is all she says. The promise came true, and she was a happy mother.

Years pass, and it is now harvest time. The boy goes out to his father, who is in the field, and has what we should call a sun-stroke. "My head, my head", he cries. He is taken home to his mother and before long dies in her arms. Remembering the circumstances of his birth, she lays the body on the spare-room bed and then goes to find Elisha, who is staying on Mount Carmel. They meet, and Elisha sees she is in great trouble and says, "The Lord hath hid it from me and hath not told me". This is a significant verse, showing that a prophet had the gift of second sight and expected to know what was happening at a distance; also that he claimed no merit for this—all was God's gift to his servant. The end of the story is familiar. Elisha returns with her, stretches himself on the boy, whose life is restored.

The charm of the passage lies in the character of the woman, who is noteworthy for her hospitality and independence. She takes the initiative in proposing to build and furnish a guest-chamber for the use of the prophet; that she gives him meals goes without saying. One of the outstanding virtues of the early Christians was that they were "given to hospitality". Inns had a bad reputation, and a Christian going to a strange city was sure to find a brother ready to put him up. Brother? Surely we must say sister, for then, as now, the burden of hospitality fell on the woman. There is no more admirable trait in women than their readiness to take on extra

48

work in order to entertain their relations and friends, however full their lives are already. Church members do more than that, so often are they asked to entertain a visiting preacher or speaker, a task which they gladly undertake.

The other feature in the woman of Shunem that we must admire is her independence. Given a chance of the king's favour and a position about the Court, she says, "I dwell among mine own people"; I prefer to stay at home. Change is good for us all, and it is necessary to make an effort to get away sometimes. But the true housewife is never happier than at home. She realizes the truth of what the old Roman poet said:

> They change their skies and not their heart
> Who haste across the sea.

So our great woman is a rebuke to those who are never happy except in perpetual motion and change, which distract us from facing the real issues of life.

19

The Chosen People

You only have I known of all the families of the earth; therefore I will visit upon you all your iniquities. AMOS 3. 2.

IF ISRAEL was the chosen people, what sort of men should we expect to find in her? A holy people, a kingdom of priests? That was the ideal. To know the reality we turn to the pages of Amos, the shepherd from the wilderness of Judah, who visited the northern kingdom some 750 years before Christ.

What a come-down it is! A doleful picture of a cruel aristocracy, heartless great ladies, dishonest traders, an oppressed poor. There are vivid details of commercial dishonesty: weights and measures are falsified and food is adulterated. Contracts are so ruthlessly enforced that, if small holders fail to pay the debts on their mortgaged property, their children are sold as slaves. Religious observances are a mockery of holy worship, the sanctuaries hotbeds of abuses. Yet the people are confident of God's favour. They are his chosen and in due course the Day of the Lord will come and vindicate them.

The stern voice of Amos pricks the bubble. God's judgement is coming, but to you it will bring punishment. The Day of the Lord will be a day of retribution for wicked people. God cares for the Hebrews, but he cares for the Syrians too; even for the Philistines, whose home in Palestine was secured by his help. All is summed up in the text. You, Israel, are my people; I have picked you out from the other nations to play a special part in history. Just because of this I will punish you for your iniquities. It is the lesson taught by Jesus: "To whomsoever much is given, of him shall much be required" (Luke 12. 48).

Now what had gone wrong? How came it that the high ideals learned from Moses had become so tarnished? The recent history of Israel provides the answer. The nation had been through what we might call an industrial revolution on a very small scale. As commerce developed the old ideas of brotherhood faded. The Hebrews had been organized by clans and families; in hard times the weaker members were looked after just because they belonged to the family. All this had gone by the board. To-day we know how to deal with such problems. The State has learned by experience and can pass and enforce the necessary laws. Inspectors prevent adulteration of food and see that weights and measures are accurate. Also, the importance of production is now realized. High wages mean high consumption, which makes the wheels of industry go round. But this has become

50

possible only thanks to scientific and technological skill. People as a whole do not work so hard but they work to better purpose. The secret has been discovered by bitter experience and was completely hidden from the Old Hebrews. The nineteenth century, when Amos was the book of the Old Testament that appealed supremely to reformers, was only feeling its way towards it. Even now there are many emergencies with which the state cannot deal, and the need for brotherhood and neighbourly kindness remains what it was in the days of Amos. Besides, we know that the evils he denounces are rooted in human nature and to a large extent are still with us, though driven underground. And we do not know how long prosperity will last. There may be unsuspected weaknesses in our system, which will cause a breakdown one day.

Old people remember the days when the British had the illusion that they were the chosen people; the British-Israel movement was a symptom of this. It reached its peak at the time of Queen Victoria's Diamond Jubilee in 1897, when Rudyard Kipling wrote his famous poem "Recessional", with the refrain, "Lest we forget". It was meant to rebuke national pride, but he permitted himself to speak of

> Such boastings as the Gentiles use,
> Or lesser breeds without the Law

which must mean that the British are the chosen people. Well, all this has passed away, and so has the British Empire as Kipling knew it. If it results in a permanent grouping of States with common ideals, comprising men of white, brown, and black skins, on an equal footing, that will be something far better than the old Empire.

But Amos was thinking mainly of a *holy* people which had become unholy. The lessons of the Old Testament concern the Church rather than the State. The Church claims to be the new Israel, in which, as St Paul says, there is neither bond nor free; all are one in Christ. And the prophet's message is for the Church to-day: it is that we should thank God for his exceeding goodness in choosing us as his people and remember the greatness of the responsibility we have incurred. To the Church more than even to ancient Israel the words apply: "To whomsoever much is given, of him shall much be required." The Church is put in a position of privilege that she may the better serve God's purposes. We are inclined sometimes to shrink from the magnitude of the burdens laid upon us, all the good causes we are expected to support. But that is what we are here for, to be the servant of all, as was Christ our Master.

20

The Way of Love

When Israel was a child, then I loved him. HOSEA 11. 1.

AMOS IS a tremendous man. As we read his book we feel a high wind blowing. He is the matchless prophet of God's righteousness and wrath. Shortly after him another prophet tried to save the northern kingdom, which was drifting into its final disaster. This was Hosea, whose book is often hard to understand, largely because the Hebrew text has been damaged in the process of copying, so that in places no clear sense can be obtained. But at least we can find his great message of love and mercy, and mercy outweighs wrath. As Christina Rossetti says in a poem about the Book of Revelation,

> Seven vials hold thy wrath, but what can hold
> thy mercy?

Hosea sees the sins of Israel as clearly as Amos, but he pleads with the guilty to repent, using beautiful figures of speech, which grow out of the beauty of his mind. It is significant that at the begining of the book we find the verse, "I will avenge the blood of Jezreel upon the house of Jehu" (1. 4). In the book of Kings we have a description of Jehu's killing off the whole house of Ahab. A sad story of cruelty, only too familiar in the ancient East, which according to Kings was enacted in obedience to God's command (2 Kings 10. 30). A century passes, and so greatly has the standard of religion risen that what was once a meritorious act is now a crime to be punished by God.

Hosea pleads with Israel to forsake Baal and serve the Lord. They have formed the disasterous opinion that the God of Israel *is* Baal and can be worshipped in the manner of Baal. This was a result of the new life in Canaan. The Hebrews after a long time in the desert came into the cultivated land and for the first time fully enjoyed the fruits of agriculture, especially the corn, wine, and oil. In their ignorance they concluded that the gods of Canaan were to be thanked for these gifts. Without rejecting the God of their fathers they thought he could be worshipped under the form of Baal. This meant that many objectionable things were taken over, things unknown to the purer religion of the desert. So Hosea pleads with the people to go back to the old ways.

His preaching took a remarkable form. You, he said, are God's bride and have been unfaithful to your husband. This was daring because it was just along the lines of mixing up sex with religion that Israel had gone astray. But his boldness was justified by success, for with wonderful purity and frankness he tells the story of his life, which he now sees has been a parable of God's dealing with Israel. Following divine guidance he married a woman who after bearing him three children left home and apparently went to one of the Baal sanctuaries, where she lived an immoral life. We cannot be certain of the details, because the actual facts and the parable run into each other. It seems as if she took this course from a perverted view of religion. Baal had given her food and so deserved some return. After a time Hosea took her back and reformed her by strict discipline. This represented God's treatment of Israel. Though she had been unfaithful he was willing to take her back. But " I will bring her into the wilderness" (2. 14). Israel must return to the desert time, when her religion was pure. There is more than a hint of the suffering to come.

However, Hosea's was not a one-track mind. This was one illustration of God's love; but there was another, that of father and child. "When Israel was a child, then I loved him, and called my son out of Egypt." It taught Ephraim to walk. When the little boy was tired, I took him up in my arms. When he fell, I healed the bruises (11. 1-3). Then the figure changes. Hosea pictures God as a man driving a cart, to which as an animal Israel is harnessed. The man helps the poor beast by pulling the cart himself with cords; he eases the yoke and feeds the weary animal.

In keeping with these tender pictures is Hosea's pleading with the people. He provides a form of prayer for them to use: "Come and let us return unto the Lord. . . . After two days will he revive us: on the third day he will raise us up and we shall live before him" (6. 1, 2). And the book ends with a call to prayer (see 14. 1-12). Take *words*, earnest prayer, with you, not bullocks to be sacrificed. Then God's mercy will come, and he will say, "I will heal their backsliding, I will love them freely: for mine anger is turned away".

Hosea's book is unque in the Bible for its tenderness and the way it uses all the resources of language to teach the lesson of God's love.

21

Isaiah's Call

Here am I; send me. ISAIAH 6. 8.

THE PROPHETS of Israel were alike in that they all received a message from God, but otherwise they differed greatly. Amos was a shepherd, Micah too was a countryman. Isaiah, on the other hand, was an important figure in the capital city of Jerusalem, in close touch with the King and the officers of State. He was not too proud to use the characteristic methods of a prophet, and on one occasion he went about the streets for three years naked and barefoot, as a sign that the Egyptians would be led away captive by the Assyrians. This means that he left off the dignified outer garment and dressed only in the tunic worn next the skin.

Isaiah's call to be a prophet is one of the most striking stories in the Bible. He was in the Temple, taking part in the worship. The house was filled with the smoke of the sacrifices and we may assume that it rang with shouts, for Hebrew worship was noisy. Suddenly the things of this world faded and heaven was opened. He saw the Lord on his throne high above, surrounded by angels. Streaming out from God was a train that filled the Temple. Some idea of Isaiah's sensations may be gathered from the Aurora Borealis, seen to perfection in the north of Scotland. The sky is a mass of flashing green lights, filling the observer with awe and wonder and suggesting the robe of Almighty God. The vision taught two great truths: God is transcendent, exalted far above man, and yet he fills the lower earth with his presence. It was a message to Isaiah and at the same time a lesson to the Church of the future. Suggested by the ordinary routine of the Temple, it revealed for a moment the reality of which our earthly worship is a shadow. Scientific men would say that Isaiah's experience was a hallucination; others present would have seen nothing out of the ordinary. Perhaps so, but it was a true hallucination, by which God was using every day things to teach spiritual truths.

The first lesson was that of the majesty and holiness of God, before whom the angels were crying, "Holy, Holy, Holy", words which have passed into the liturgy of the Church, being found in both the Communion Service and the Te Deum. The main idea in the word "holy" is of something apart from sinful man, before which we abase ourselves in utter humility. A true vision has this effect; if a vision puffs up the recipient, it is likely to be the devil disguising himself as an angel of light. So Isaiah was humbled to the dust, feeling the burden of corporate sins as well as his own. "Woe is me!" he cried, "I am a man of unclean lips, and I dwell in the midst of a people of unclean lips!" Then came his cleansing, in terms suggested by the apparatus of the Temple. An angel took a burning coal from the altar and touched his lips with it saying, "Thine iniquity is taken away, and thy sin is purged".

Next came a voice from heaven. "Whom shall I send, and who will go for us?" To which Isaiah replied in utter humility, but with trust that God would give the needed strength, "Here am I; send me".

Clearly such an account of first-hand spiritual experience could never have been invented. It puts into human words an act of God which far surpassed the power of man to describe fully. None of us is likely to have so shattering and yet up-lifting a vision. The chapter lives on as the classic account of heaven opened and its power descending upon man. Everything is here. First the vision of God in his glory. Then the unworthiness of man and its cleansing by God's mercy. Then the call to work in the vineyard and man's answer to the call.

Now this superb story of God's revelation of himself and man's response is based on the foundation of everyday worship. May the experience come to us at least once or twice in a lifetime of realizing what worship really is—the lifting up of our hearts into the heavens, where God's voice is clearly heard, so that we return to earth nerved and inspired for the daily round of human existence, ready for new ventures and saying "Here am I; send me".

22

The Messiah

Unto us a child is born, unto us a son is given. ISAIAH 9. 6.

THE FAMOUS passages in the Old Testament about the Messiah are mostly found in Isaiah. Before considering them, let us ask what "Messiah" means. It is simply the Hebrew word for "anointed". Translated into Greek it becomes "Christ". Kings in the Old Testament were set apart for their office by anointing, so Messiah means "anointed king".

The centuries passed, and a king descended from David was still on the throne at Jerusalem; the fame and sanctity of the Davidic king had grown continually. The reigning monarch was often unsatisfactory, and the people's hopes were transferred to the ideal cherished in their hearts. The hope persisted that one day the ideal king would reign, God's chosen one, faithfully fulfilling the divine purpose and giving peace and prosperity and justice to Judah. The more they were disappointed, the more their hopes and beliefs were set in the future, when the true "Son of David" would come.

When Isaiah was still a young man, Judah was attacked by two little States north of her land—Israel with Samaria and Syria with Damascus as their capitals. They were trying to force Judah to be their ally against the mighty Assyria. It was

57

a hopeless policy, and Isaiah said, "Have nothing to do with such folly". He predicted that the fire would soon burn itself out. A sign of deliverance would be given to king Ahaz (see 7. 14-16). A virgin, or young woman, would conceive and bear a son, and call his name Immanuel, which means "God is with us". By the time the boy was old enough to distinguish between good and bad food, that is within two or three years, the enemy armies would have withdrawn and normal food would be available; "butter and honey shall he eat". The word which we translate "virgin" need not mean more than a young woman and in this passage may mean just any woman who has a child now. If the passage stood alone we should be reluctant to draw out of it more than this.

But Isaiah elsewhere describes the ideal king of the future in such glowing terms that it is difficult to explain away the Immanuel passage. In chapter 9 we find: "Unto us a child is born, unto us a son is given . . . and his name shall be called Wonderful Councillor, mighty Hero (this seems to be the best translation), Everlasting Father (of his people), Prince of Peace." And this child will sit on the throne of David.

The third passage develops the theme further. "There shall come up a shoot out of the stock of Jesse" (11. 1). This means that the royal line of David will come to an end, for a time; the tree will be cut down and only the stump left. But from the stump will spring a new shoot. The monarchy of David's line will be revived and the promised king will fulfil all hopes. He will have the gifts of the Spirit, with which to judge the people wisely. In his time peace and happiness will prevail. Even the beasts of the field will lay aside their fierceness. "The wolf shall dwell with the lamb . . . the calf and the young lion together"; a young lad will lead them. The idea is Paradise Regained. The conditions of the Garden of Eden will return, as when Adam sat fearless among the animals and give them their names. And the whole earth will be "full of the knowledge of the Lord".

No wonder the early Christians found Jesus in these chapters and Emmanuel became one of his titles. Exactly how much Isaiah meant by his prophecy of the Virgin we can never know, but in the light of the other two passages we are justified in seeing some mystery in his words beyond the birth of an ordinary child.

Seven hundred years passed, and the Messiah came to the Jewish Church; but only a few of "his own" received him. So the Gentiles became heirs of the promises. Untold blessings flowed from the birth in human form of the Son of God, even though Isaiah's prophecies were not fulfilled literally. The Christians indeed experienced a new creation and a return to the happiness of Eden, but it was spiritual, in their hearts, not displayed in earthly splendour. They and their successors have had to continue in the way of struggle and hardship. But Isaiah's glowing words remain to inspire us with an undying hope of a better land.

23

In the Day of Trouble

Thus saith the Lord . . . I will defend this city to save it, for mine own sake, and for my servant David's sake.
ISAIAH 37. 33, 35.

THE NEW TESTAMENT gives us little help in understanding the political issues of our time, for it is the book of the Church; the early Christians had all they could do to survive. For guidance as to God's dealing with States we must turn to the Old Testament, and especially to the prophets. Among these Isaiah is outstanding, for he was a confidant of kings and helped to decide their policy.

A great crisis befell Judah in the later years of Isaiah, when Sennacherib, king of Assyria, invaded the land. A few miles to the north was Samaria, now a province of the Assyrian empire; to the south was a strip of desert, and then Egypt. Sennacherib's objective was of course Egypt, whose army came to meet him in the country near Gaza. But he also ravaged Judah and sent an embassy to summon Jerusalem to surrender. The envoys spoke to the people on the walls in the Hebrew language: their God was powerless to deliver them, and they had better surrender at once and secure favourable terms. Hezekiah the king sent messengers to Isaiah, bidding him pray for the people in their trouble, which he did. Then came a formal letter from Sennacherib to Hezekiah, repeating the message already given orally.

We now get a charming touch. Hezekiah goes to the Temple and spreads out the letter before the Lord (it would be in the form of a roll which would have to be unfolded) and prays for help. Here is a piece of practical religion. When we get an important letter, the answer to which needs thought, let us spread it before the Lord and get his help. This will, if nothing else, often save us from an angry reply.

Isaiah with splendid faith assured Hezekiah that God was on his side. The arrogance of Assyria would be punished. This was not the act of a fanatic; he knew that Judah had resources. The old saying, "Trust in God and keep your powder dry", applied then. Hezekiah had carried out a wonderful piece of engineering. The water supply of Jerusalem came mainly from the Virgin's Spring, just outside the eastern wall. He had a tunnel made through the solid rock, 1,700 feet long, which diverted the water to the pool of Siloam inside the city. So far as water went, Jerusalem could stand a siege, whereas the besieging army would have difficulty in getting any. Also he knew that Sennacherib had his hands full with his chief enemy Egypt and would not wish to be diverted. How deliverance would come Isaiah could not know, but he made the venture of faith and was content to leave the issue in God's hands.

As it happened, a disaster befell the Assyrian army. The Bible describes it in famous words. "The angel of the Lord went forth and smote in the army of the Assyrians a hundred and four score and five thousand (185,000 in all): and when they arose early in the morning, behold, they were all dead corpses." The Greek historian Herodotus ascribes the disaster to mice. Remembering that bubonic plague is spread by the parasites which rats and mice harbour, also the ignorance of modern methods of hygiene which would make an ancient camp in a hot climate very unhealthy, it is a reasonable guess that a large part of the army died of disease.

Isaiah was always far-sighted. We read that the leader of a resistance movement in Babylon, by name Merodach-Baladan, sent to Jerusalem, evidently to get allies against Assyria, and Hezekiah showed him all his military strength. Isaiah rebuked him, saying that, if Babylon overthrew Assyria, it would be as much a danger and would carry the Jews away into captivity.

The sequel to the story of Hezekiah and Isaiah is significant. The Jews were convinced that God would always preserve Jerusalem, and a century later, when Nebuchadnezzar came, were sure that it would escape the disaster that had befallen Samaria and the Northern Kingdom. In other words, they presumed on God, and the task of the later prophets was to disabuse them of false notions. The same lesson applies to the modern world. No nation can count on continual success. God in his almighty wisdom "putteth down one and setteth up another".

24

Jeremiah (i)

I have found the book of the law in the house of the Lord.
2 KINGS 22. 8.

IS IT possible to interest a congregation to-day in Jeremiah? Let us at least try. We must begin by sketching the background of his life, which was Jerusalem in the years before and after 600 B.C. Everything is on a tiny scale, but that does not matter. We study ancient Athens partly for its own sake and partly because it is a working model of politics to-day. Most of our modern words describing government—aristocracy, democracy, oligarchy, politics itself—and even devices like voting were invented there. Similarly, little Jerusalem, with a territory stretching four or five miles to the north and twenty-five to thirty on the east, south, and west, is a laboratory in which we can watch God's dealings with the human soul.

First we must think of the pious young king Josiah and his reformation carried out in the year 621. This consisted of getting rid of the heathen elements in popular religion and turning out the Assyrian emblems put in the Temple by his grandfather Manasseh. Now Manasseh was the prize villain of Jewish history. But the poor man could not help himself. He was a vassal or satellite of the great Assyrian empire and had to show his loyalty by putting objects of Assyrian worship in the Temple; for example, the horses of the Sun, which according to the myth drew the chariot of the sun-god across the sky from east to west. By 621 the Assyrian empire was crumbling, and that Josiah was able to purge out heathenism was due to this; he could now assert nationalism and the national religion without bringing retribution on himself.

In this critical year a full-scale restoration of the Temple was proceeding. As happens sometimes to-day, lost things turn up when a church is being restored, as they do in the house at spring-cleaning. The king, who looked on the Temple as a kind of private chapel, had to be informed of progress, so Hilkiah the high priest sent Shaphan to him with the latest news. When Shaphan had reported he added, "By the way, we've found the book of the law".

Now this book was none other than the one we call Deuteronomy. How long it had existed no one knows, but when discovered it came as a startling novelty. Most scholars think that it was an old code of law rewritten by prophets to give the teaching of Moses in a modern form. There is no doubt of its identity; the special features of the reformation as described in 2 Kings are the new laws which appear in Deuteronomy and are not found in Exodus, Leviticus or Numbers. The obvious difficulty is that they are put in the mouth of Moses, who lived 600 to 700 years before. To those who are familiar with the Hebrew mind this is not a difficulty, for in a way hard for us to understand the Hebrews abolished the distinction between past and present. Abraham was a real person to later ages, living on in his sons. So was Moses, who gave the Law, a living force, and later editions of the Law as Deuteronomy were ascribed to him in perfect good faith— this is what he would have said if he had been alive to-day.

The special means which Josiah took to reform popular religion were startling. All the local high places, the shrines on neighbouring hill tops where from time immemorial the villagers had offered sacrifices, were destroyed. Everything had to be centralized at Jerusalem and done under the eye of the King. Even Passover, the family festival, since the Exodus the prerogative of the father of the family, was allowed only in the Temple. Such a revolution would have been impossible in any but a tiny country. Even so, it meant that country people had no services except at the three great feasts of Passover, Pentecost, and Tabernacles. Think of the hardships inflicted on the priests. The poor country parsons were disestablished and disendowed. The first idea was to bring them to Jerusalem and let them share in the offerings made there, but the Temple priests, the Cathedral clergy as we might say, objected. In spite of difficulties the reformation went through and people were "made good by Act of Parliament". Were they really? That is what we must discover from Jeremiah.

All the time an inspired young man, Jeremiah himself, was watching the experiment, at first it seems with approving eyes; but later he saw its weak points. For see what was happening. Old sanctities and traditions were ruthlessly destroyed. In the well-meant effort to reform the old religion much good was sacrificed. The people were filled with a glow of self-satisfaction at what they had done and expected to be rewarded by prosperity. When, instead, disaster came their morale was shattered and they fell back into heathenism. Most serious of all, the Jews were taught to put their faith in institutional religion, and especially in the Temple, at a time when it was about to be destroyed.

But God raised up the superb man Jeremiah to teach them a deeper and more spiritual religion.

25

Jeremiah (ii)

Is this house, which is called by my name, become a den of robbers in your eyes? Behold I, even I, have seen it, saith the Lord. JEREMIAH 7. 11.

LAST TIME we thought about the reformation of Jewish religion carried out by the young King Josiah. One might have thought that never had a nation so seriously set to work to cast out evil and do good. But it cost more to redeem their souls. Can any nation be made good by Government action? In fact, the very measures taken to promote religion produced a new crop of evils which needed to be cast out. This at least was the conviction of Jeremiah, whom God raised up to deal with the crisis.

Let us see how God called him. Jeremiah had a series of visions—simply homely things such as he had often seen before, but now he was inspired to find in them a spiritual meaning. In mid-winter he noticed an almond-tree in blossom. In England this flowers in March, in Palestine in January. The other trees were still bare, seemingly asleep, but the almond was awake. (The Hebrew word for it means "watcher", the tree which is awake when the others are asleep.) In a flash the illumination came. God has not gone to sleep: he is the divine watcher whose eyes are on the sins of Judah and who will punish her for them (1. 11, 12). Then Jeremiah saw a cauldron filled with water, over a fire. The wind was blowing from the north, and the steam was drifting in a southerly direction. This he realized stood for the coming of an invading army from the north, to be God's agent of punishment (1. 13-16).

Once more, he felt an impulse to visit a potter's shop, where pottery was both made and sold. He must have seen the process scores of times, but never before had it yielded a spiritual lesson. He watched the man manipulating the wet clay; one piece was spoiled and thrown aside. Then the potter picked it up and remodelled it according to his will (18. 1-4). This was a picture of the absolute power of God, but it also taught a lesson about God's action on the hearts of men. His first plan breaks down owing to their wilful obstinacy, but he does not despair; rather, he tries again and makes a new plan for their lives. How often we have proved this in our own experience! Our failure, which at the time seemed disastrous, by God's mercy has been overruled for good; indeed an initial failure seems to have been part of God's plan for our lives. So in Jeremiah's case: his failure to influence the people led to the ultimate success of his teaching, and the failure of Josiah's reformation paved the way to the Jews' learning the lesson of inner spiritual religion, as we see so wonderfully in some of the Psalms. Notice that the idea of the visions is the same as we see in our Lord's parables, in which he draws lessons from Nature; there is one God, whose working may be traced both in the natural order and in the kingdom of grace.

The message received by Jeremiah, at least at first, was always the same: God is about to judge the wicked nation. Judah was no worse than other nations, but she had a light denied to them, to which she had proved herself unfaithful. Jeremiah, who was as patriotic by nature as any other man, was overwhelmed with sorrow at the news he had to deliver. Here are some of his outcries:

"Oh that my head were waters, and mine eyes a fountain of tears, that I might weep day and night for the slain of the daughter of my people" (9. 1).

"Hast thou utterly rejected Judah? Hath thy soul loathed Zion? Why hast thou smitten us, and there is no healing for us?" (14. 19).

"Why is my pain perpetual, and my wound incurable, which refuseth to be healed?" (15. 18).

"Cursed be the day wherein I was born . . . cursed be the man who brought tidings to my father, saying, A man child is born unto thee; making him very glad" (20. 14, 15).

Jeremiah does not mind standing up to God and expostulating, as Job does. This is a test of true revelation, that it is unwelcome, and there is no suspicion of wishful thinking. The other prophets ("false prophets" we call them in the light of events, but at the time it was natural to believe them) proclaimed prosperity and a continuance of independence, as a reward for the nation's taking religion seriously and abolishing abuses. Jeremiah had to stand alone, against the stream. Note, too, that there was nothing mechanical in the revelation; nothing to suggest that he was merely a channel for God's word. Before he delivered it to the people he had received it into himself, digested it, and made it his own. As he says, "thy words were found, and I did eat them" (15. 16).

Remember what the reformation had done. The village sanctuaries, the old high places, were suppressed, and worship was concentrated in the Temple. Any holiness it had formerly possessed in the minds of the people was greatly enhanced now. How dreadful it must have been to break down the people's belief in their religion! At first it seems that Jeremiah, as always obeying the divine leading, engaged in a mission in which he preached the reformed religion in the capital and the country towns (11. 6). But when he saw that the morals of the people were no better he took the momentous decision to denounce institutional religion: good in its way, it becomes a hindrance to the Kingdom of God if people were content with it alone. Deuteronomy is a noble book. It proclaims a high moral standard, sustained by love and gratitude to God for his mercies. The tragedy was that the people neglected its positive and spiritual side.

Jeremiah began with the Temple. God's holy house, it had become "a den of robbers", to which those who oppressed the poor retired to digest their ill-gotten gains (7. 11). Those who said with a mixture of patriotism and unction, as they looked on the shrine, "The Temple of the Lord, the Temple of the Lord, the Temple of the Lord, are these (buildings)", were speaking lying words (7. 4). Even the Ark of the Covenant with its hallowed associations had become an abuse. "They shall say no more, The ark of the covenant of the Lord; neither shall it come to mind" (3. 16). Sacrifices too, which had been offered from time immemorial, were not required.

Was there ever a more cruel fate? To be obliged to tell the people to burn what they had adored and to unlearn their deepest convictions! We may well believe that he overstated his case, and that outward observances are the natural expression of inward religion, but we must also believe that his message was the word of God for that moment in human history.

26

Jeremiah (iii)

Seek ye the peace of the city whither I have caused you to be carried away captive, and pray unto the Lord for it: for in the peace thereof shall ye have peace. JEREMIAH 29. 7.

LAST TIME we left Jeremiah protesting against the attempt to save Judah by enforcing strict laws about religion. This was his message for nearly forty years; he hated having to deliver it, but there was no alternative, he must obey God. The other part of his message was the coming of judgement upon a guilty nation. He actually counselled submission to a foreign power: Babylon, which conquered Assyria in the year 612, was to be accepted as master. He used no arguments but simply announced the bare fact of God's will. It says much for the Jews that he escaped with his life; in modern times any one who favoured the enemy's cause in time of war as Jeremiah did would in most countries be shot. Looking back on this period we can see that he was raised up by God to teach the people that they could live a religious life without the Temple or sacrifices; but those whose lot is cast in a time of crisis cannot be expected to see round the corner.

Let us now look at two other revelations that the prophet received.

The first is indeed terrible. "I beheld the earth, and, lo, it was waste and void; and the heavens, and they had no light"

(4. 23-5). The birds had all fled, no men were left, the land was a desolation. "Waste and void", *tohu wa bohu* in Hebrew, the phrase used at the beginning of Genesis, there translated "without form and void", to describe the primeval chaos. (*Tohu-bohu* is found in both French and German, meaning confusion and desolation.) Jeremiah's mission was to pull down and destroy, before he could build up. How complete the desolation was to be these words illustrate. Earth has to return to its state before creation in order to prepare the way for a new creation. This is of course the language of poetry, but so far as desolation goes it was not exaggerated, for the Babylonians in their second attack on Jerusalem in 586 destroyed almost everything.

The second revelation was when God commanded Jeremiah not to marry. Only two other Jews do we know in the Bible who abstained from marriage on grounds of principle—Jesus himself and St Paul. The latter in his First Epistle to the Corinthians says he wishes all men were unmarried like himself. His reason is "the present distress", by which he means the sufferings about to come on the world, which are worse for the family man. So Jeremiah is taught that private joys are out of place when public sufferings are so great (16. 1). The joys of marriage are to be eschewed, so too is sympathy with mourners; he is not even to attend funerals. Indeed he must hold himself aloof from all earthly entanglements, that he may be free to hear God's voice and do whatever he is told.

We now turn to the history of the time. In 608 Pharaoh, King of Egypt, marched through Palestine with an army in order to assert Egypt's rights. The balance of power had been upset by the rise of Babylonia, which took the place of Assyria. Pharaoh, who did not want a strong Israel on his frontier (how modern it sounds!), summoned Josiah to account for his actions and put him to death. This was a terrible blow to the morale of the Jews. Having reformed religion, they expected to be rewarded by God—and this was what they got! So they relapsed into their old ways and brought back the objects of foreign worship. This may be described as an act of spiritual reinsurance. They did not mean to desert their God, but it was politic to keep on the right side of these powerful foreign gods, who had shown themselves stronger than the God of the Jews.

Then in 597 Nebuchadnezzar, King of Babylon, attacked Jerusalem. Jehoiachin, the young king, submitted and was taken prisoner to Babylon with about 2,000 prominent men. He was treated reasonably well. Some years ago a German scholar, working through a pile of thousands of cuneiform tablets, to his surprise came across Jehoiachin's ration card, entitling him to a fixed allowance of so much corn, wine, and oil a day. Meanwhile Judah remained independent in a sense under its last king Zedekiah, who tried to play Egypt off against Babylonia. Nebuchadnezzar came again, and in 586 destroyed Jerusalem and its Temple, also the country towns of Judah, and took many more of the inhabitants into exile.

The book of Jeremiah ends with a pathetic scene in Egypt where a number of Jews have fled, taking the prophet with them. They reproach him for leading them astray. What good has his religion done them? In the old days, when they worshipped the Queen of Heaven, all went well. So Jeremiah's life and ministry end, in hopeless failure it seems. How strong his influence was to prove we shall see next time.

Before the capture of the city Jeremiah wrote a remarkable letter to the first group of exiles in Babylon. It is the earliest example of spiritual teaching given in the form of a letter, and it points the way to the Epistles of St Paul (chapter 29). The Jews went into exile in despair, thinking that true religion was impossible outside the Holy Land and with no Holy Temple. They could not offer sacrifices, what was left for them to do? Jeremiah tells them to settle down in the strange land, marry, bring up children, build houses, cultivate the land. When prophets tell them to expect speedy deliverance they must not believe it. Deliverance will come at long last, after seventy years. That is a round number, meaning something like, "You won't see it, nor your children, but your grand-children will". Further, they must identify themselves with Babylon, seek its well-being, and pray to God for their heathen rulers: "Seek the peace of the city whither I have caused you to be carried away captive, and pray unto the Lord God for it: for in the peace thereof shall ye have peace."

This is the principle that is worked out in the New Testament. "Render unto Caesar the things that are Caesar's, says Jesus. "Let every soul be subject unto the higher powers", says St Paul. Most striking of all, St Peter says, "Honour the King", when apparently Nero was on the throne. In many countries Christians are in a minority, perhaps a tiny minority. When our fellow Christians in Russia, China, and elsewhere support the government of their country they have the authority of the Bible behind them.

27

Jeremiah (iv)

Who do men say that the Son of Man is? They said, some say . . . Jeremiah. MATTHEW 16. 13, 14.

WE LEFT Jeremiah at the end of his life to all appearances a complete failure. Now we see how outstanding he was—Christ was thought by some to be Jeremiah come to life again. We will return to this presently. There are two earlier signs of his prestige that deserve to be mentioned. The first is the book of Lamentations, which was not written by Jeremiah but comes from the disheartened group of Jews left in Jerusalem when the leaders of the nation were taken to Babylon. If the prophet was not listened to in his lifetime, when his words became true and disaster fell on the Jews they repented on a national scale. The whole book of Lamentations is one long cry of repentance—we have sinned, and we accept our well-deserved punishment. "It is of the Lord's mercies that we are not consumed . . . they are new every morning". (Lam. 3. 22, 23). The other example comes in the second book of Maccabees (15. 14). Judas Maccabaeus tells his soldiers a dream he has had. It is only a dream, but dreams grow out of men's minds and, especially then, were real things. "A man of venerable age and exceeding glory, and wonderful and most majestic was the dignity around him." In his dream the holy high priest Onias, now dead, says: "This is the lover of the brethren, he who prayeth much for the people and the holy city, Jeremiah the prophet of God."

But the most remarkable tributes come from the New Testament. There is the opinion of the people that Jesus was Jeremiah come to life. Far more important are our Lord's words in the Upper Room, when he uses the sentence we know so well, "This is my blood of the New Covenant (or Testament), which is shed for you and for many for the remission of sins". The first Covenant was made at the foot of Mount Sinai, when Moses took the blood of a sacrificed bullock and threw part of it on the altar and part on the people. The altar represented God, and so God and the people were joined by the blood shared between them. It was not a magical charm but involved a moral decision on the part of the people, who promised to obey the laws given by God through Moses. God's part in the pact was to love and protect his people; he could not be bound by an oath but only by his own nature; they could trust his "loving kindness". Thus early in the Bible do we find salvation by faith (Ex. 24).

The culmination of Jeremiah's ministry was when he prophesied a new covenant, not sealed in blood like the old one, but "this is the covenant that I will make with the house of Israel after those days, saith the Lord. I will put my law in their inward parts, and in their heart will I write it . . . they shall all know me from the least of them unto the greatest of them" (31. 33, 34). The prophecy could not be fulfilled at that time. When the Jews returned from exile, the Temple was rebuilt and sacrifice restored. The old ways had too strong a hold to be changed. But with marvellous God-given insight Jeremiah saw what the future of religion was to be.

In the Upper Room Jesus combined the two covenants, of Moses and Jeremiah, and made a final one, far greater than either. Blood could not be dispensed with; but this time it was the blood of the God-man, not of an animal. The red wine stood for his blood that was to be poured out in his Passion, the giving of life by an agonizing death. But the old limitation to the house of Israel was removed. This time it was "for you and for many", that is in Hebrew idiom the whole human race; as when Jesus said he would give his life "a ransom for many"—for Israel first and then to be passed on to all. And it is to be the New Covenant foretold by Jeremiah, in which God through Christ will speak directly to the hearts of all. As we know, the ordinances of the Church are sacred, for they are God's gift, but God can dispense with them if he thinks fit, and the believer can commune direct with his Saviour.

This problem of institutional religion was first raised by Jeremiah. He was dealing with a people who had been taught that for communion with God it was necessary to go to one holy spot, the Temple at Jerusalem, and, he was convinced, would soon have to do without Temple and Sanctuary, and even without sacrifices, which all agreed were necessary. For they were to be exiled to a foreign land, where according to the ideas of the time they could not offer sacrifice, because it did not belong to their God. Divinely inspired, he taught that God was greater than any ordinances of religion, and

73

would be with his people, however far they were from the central sanctuary. There they could live a decent life and keep at least part of the Law. The rest they could safely leave in God's hands. Jeremiah could not see the mystery hidden in the future, that sacrifice would still be needed, but not that of a dumb animal. Rather, the loving heart of a fellow human being, himself God, was to be pierced. And from this sacrifice would spring the Christian Sacrifice, in which the assembly of faithful people would join and till the end of the world would commemorate the Cross of Calvary, lovingly identifying themselves with it and offering their own selves, their souls and bodies, to be a living sacrifice to God. This was to be the outward sign of the New Covenant.

The Eucharist is the perfect harmonizing of outward and inward religion. It requires the simplest of outward forms, a taste of bread and a sip of wine, though a right instinct bids us clothe the simplicity with dignity and even splendour. The holiest priest cannot receive the Bread of Life unless some one is there to receive with him, perhaps a newly confirmed schoolboy who acts as server. All the time we are reminded that the action is corporate and we depend on fellow-members of the Church. But what the Sacrament means to the faithful communicant is a secret between him and his Lord.

This wonder of inner religion is illustrated elsewhere in the Old Testament, especially in the Psalms, but humanly speaking it goes back to the revelation given by God to his servant Jeremiah.

28

National Repentance

It is of the Lord's mercies that we are not consumed . . .
they are new every morning. LAMENTATIONS 3. 22-3.

SEVERAL TIMES in its long history Jerusalem has had to
pass through a period of agony. The first of these ordeals is
described in the book of Lamentations. Elsewhere we read the
bare facts of the fall of the city at the hands of Nebuchadnezzar, King of Babylon; here we have the heart's outpouring
of those who survived, and who even in the depth of misery
could produce fine poetry.

When in the year 586 B.C. the city fell, the blow seemed
final. Nebuchadnezzar, who as ancient conquerors went was
not too bad, determined to make a thorough job of it. Not
only the capital but also the smaller towns of Judah were
destroyed. The people divided into three groups. A considerable number fled into Egypt, taking with them the
prophet Jeremiah, in whose pages we find them complaining
of their treatment at God's hands; they would have done
better to worship the Queen of Heaven, as in olden days. The
most important part, in quality if not in quantity, were taken
to Babylonia; they included the royal family, the nobles, and
the priests. They were probably put to work at first in com-
pulsory labour camps, but later seem to have prospered. The
world then was as full of displaced persons as it is now; the
Jews at least rose above their difficulties.

The largest number, however, remained in their own land
and managed to survive in spite of the destruction of the
State. The sting of the disaster lay just in this: they had so
identified their cause with that of their God that they felt
safe; for his own credit's sake he would not let them down.
As it was, the bottom had dropped out of their world. Had

there been a moral and spiritual collapse we should not have been surprised and certainly should not have blamed them.

What in fact do we find? When we are punished, the natural reaction is to make excuses: at least, we say, we did not deserve all that. The same applies to nations; they too justify themselves and, if only out of loyalty to their country, say that the punishment exceeds the crime. But these wonderful Jews provide perhaps the only example in history of a penitent nation bowed in utter humility under the hand of Almighty God.

Their plight was terrible. "Jerusalem remembereth in the days of her afflictions and her miseries all her pleasant things that were from the days of old . . . Jerusalem hath grievously sinned; therefore she is become as an unclean thing" (1. 7, 8). "All that pass by . . . hiss and wag their head at the daughter of Jerusalem, saying, Is this the city that men called The perfection of beauty, The joy of the whole earth?" (2. 15). But "The Lord is righteous; for I have rebelled against his commandment" (1. 18). And we are alive, thanks to the mercy of God! "It is of the Lord's mercies that we are not consumed, because his compassions fail not. They are new every morning" (3. 22, 23). We can rely on his goodness: "The Lord will not cast off for ever . . . He doth not afflict willingly the children of men" (3. 31, 33). And we know that there is a purpose behind all our sufferings: "It is good that a man should hope and quietly wait for the salvation of the Lord. It is good for a man that he bear the yoke in his youth" (3. 26, 27). Note the confidence that the history of Israel is still in its early stages. Meanwhile let us continue to repent and "let us lift up our hearts with our hands unto God in the heavens" (3. 41)—words that have been taken into the liturgy with its cry, "Lift up your hearts: We lift them up unto the Lord".

Finally in these words of utter despair which cannot relinquish hope we find sentences which the Church has taken as foretelling the Passion of the Son of God. "Is it nothing to you, all ye that pass by? Behold and see if their be any sorrow like unto my sorrow" (1. 12). "Remember my affliction and my misery, the wormwood and the gall" (3. 19).

What lessons of penitence and hope are taught by this little-read and at first sight depressing book of the Bible!

29

Ezekiel's Wife

I will take away from thee the desire of thine eyes with a stroke . . . and at even my wife died. EZEKIEL. 24. 16, 18. One that had escaped from Jerusalem came unto me, saying, The city is smitten. EZEKIEL 33. 21.

THE BOOK of Ezekiel is long and bewildering, and few of the laity make any attempt to understand it. I shall try to make you see him as a fascinating personality and, as an experiment, to suppose that his wife is telling the story to a reporter, at a date shortly before the news of the fall of Jerusalem reached the exiles in Babylonia.

My husband and I came here eleven years ago with our good young king Jehoiachin and many others, when the Babylonians carried us away from Jerusalem after the city had surrendered (1. 2; 2 Kings 24. 15). We were away from the main body at first, in a little settlement by the River Chebar (1. 3), but before long we joined them and made our

---

[1] This sermon was suggested by an essay written for me by Miss F. Privett on the subject, "Ezekiel as I have known him. By his wife. An article contributed to the Tel Aviv *Sunday Times*". The references are added for the benefit of readers who may want to verify the details.

home at Tel-abib (3. 15). Like everyone else we miss the hills of Judaea and long to be back in our beloved homeland; but we must not complain, things might be much worse.

You want to know what it is like to live with a prophet. None too easy, as you may imagine. Ezekiel is a queer man and, as I shall tell you presently, has his moods and does unusual things. None the less it is a privilege to have such a man as a husband. As you know, he is a priest (1. 3) and sorely misses the services of the Temple, but God has made it up to him.

I vividly remember the day when the call came to him to be a prophet (1 and 2). I saw nothing and heard nothing, but he later told me as much as I could understand. He was struck dumb and didn't speak for days (3. 15, 26). He saw the Lord God who dwells invisibly on Mount Zion, here, in this far-off land. It was a vision of something tremendous, the living creatures of Nature bearing up a platform which meant the sky, and on the platform was a throne and the glory of God himself. And then he heard a voice calling him to be a prophet to the people of Israel. He would find them hard-hearted and rebellious but must continue witnessing all his life, if necessary; he had to be a watchman (3. 17), always on the look out and warning the heedless folk. Of course he accepted the call; bitter though the experience would be, it was God's will and therefore sweet (3. 3).

His immediate problem was this. The Jews, whether here or in Jerusalem, are quite sure that their city will never fall; it is the earthly home of God and for his own sake he can't let it go. They have heard the prophets of woe so often that they have become Gospel-hardened, as you might say. "It will last our time", is their view (12. 22-7). Ezekiel tells them they are wrong, using both words and actions.

Let me tell you of some of his queer doings. Once he took a sharp knife and cut off his hair and beard; the hairs meant the people who would be slain (5. 1-4). I have seen him lying on the ground and making models in the sand of Jerusalem and the enemy's camp. Sometimes he observes a kind of fast, eating and drinking siege rations (4. 9-11, 16). Perhaps the most upsetting experience I have had was when he acted the present King Zedekiah trying to escape out of the doomed city (12. 3-7). He made a hole in the wall and carried the furniture out through it by night. It was annoying to have such a mess and disturbance. But, if you live with a man of God, you must put up with these things. He has his tender side; it is nice to have him call me "the desire of mine eyes" (24. 16). I believe in him and have never complained.

You ask why he is so certain he is right. Well, God has given him terrible visions of the goings on in the Temple, the apostasy and sheer idolatry (ch. 8). He doesn't think, he *knows* what the result will be. You may wonder why the people here are blamed. It is because, though they are sad and depressed, they are not penitent. It is not our fault, they say, but we are punished for the sins of our fathers (18. 2). God is unfair, they complain, and Ezekiel has to tell them that each generation is punished for its own sins (18. 25).

I can't say they don't listen, for they enjoy his sermons. In the evening when work is done they say, "Come along and hear Ezekiel", as if he was a minstrel singing to his instrument; but they do nothing about it (33. 30-2). They are a queer lot, some of them. Fancy! the women take pillow-slips to catch the wandering souls of people asleep (13. 18).

If only they knew what Ezekiel knows! That God has not left them. He is here in this foreign land, "a sanctuary for a little while", where they can take refuge (11. 16). The dear man doesn't like being so severe. He is longing for the time when he can change his tone and speak words of comfort. When it comes he will tell of God's tender mercies. He has never lost hope that we shall go home eventually. He is planning all the time how we shall live then and be governed, with God as the Good Shepherd (34. 11), and a prince under

79

him. He has worked out plans for the rebuilding of the Temple (chs. 40—48), which will be a fountain of grace to all men (47. 1-12).

I am glad to have had this opportunity of telling what I know. It may prove to have been my last chance of doing so. My health is poor, and I am sure to die first. But I know that Ezekiel will receive strength to carry his commission through to the end.

．　．　．　．　．　．

"I will take away from thee the desire of thine eyes with a stroke. . . . At even my wife died."

30

Ezekiel the Psychic

The spirit lifted me up and took me away. EZEKIEL 3. 14.

EZEKIEL MUST have been the most remarkable psychic in the history of the world, if we may take the Bible story literally. The text tells us how he went to preach to the Jews exiled in Babylonia after God had called him to be a prophet. "The spirit lifted me up and took me away." Does this mean that he was lifted up in the air bodily and carried to another place (Tel-abib was the name of the Jewish camp)? Or is it not rather to be taken as poetry suggesting that Ezekiel was drawn by an overpowering influence to take the journey? Perhaps the truth is something in between. The prophet may have walked, but in such a state of ecstasy that he did not know what he was doing; with surprise he woke up and found himself at Tel-abib.

But look at Chapter 8 and something more remarkable is described. Ezekiel is transported by the spirit to the Temple at Jerusalem. There he sees all the wickedness practised in the name of religion. Heathen gods are worshipped, by Jews who think that their God has deserted them and that they had better be on the safe side and honour the foreign gods who have proved their power. He actually sees men looking east and worshipping the rising sun, their backs turned to the Temple to show that they repudiate the God of Israel. The purpose of showing all this to Ezekiel is to prove that judgement must fall on the guilty city of Jerusalem; their God cannot make it his home any longer. Finally Ezekiel returns in the spirit in the same way as he went and tells the exiles what he has seen; "The spirit lifted me up, and brought me *in the vision*" (11. 24). The Bible means that he really saw these things, though his ordinary body remained behind in Babylonia.

Not very long ago such a story would not have been taken seriously by educated men. At least they would have said that it could not be taken literally and must be merely a poetical way of describing the imaginations of Ezekiel's heart. But there are many things happening to-day that help us to accept the story as it stands. I refer to the study of telepathy and clairvoyance. Telepathy means communicating with friends at a distance without using the five senses. Most of us have had the experience of thinking that we must write to a friend of whom we have heard nothing for six months or more, and then our letters cross. He (or more often she, for women are more susceptible to these influences) has thought of us at the same time and written a letter. With some people the experience goes deeper than it does in such a trivial matter. A mother has an overwhelming conviction that something has gone wrong with her child, and presently she learns that the feeling was true.

Clairvoyance means seeing things at a distance as Ezekiel did. There are psychics who, on being handed an article such as a watch which belongs to an absent person unknown to them, can tell you many true things about the person. These matters have been put on a scientific basis in recent years by millions of experiments in card-guessing. Someone turns up cards by means of a machine, being unable to see them himself, and another person in a room perhaps miles away describes the card and a skilled worker takes down his call. His mind learns in ways outside the five senses, and he often gives the right answer in an astonishing way. Sometimes the mathematical odds are a million to one against getting so good a score.

It is important to remember that such things are not in themselves spiritual or religious; they come from powers of the mind which science is only now beginning to study. But in one way they do help religion. Just when scientists are showing their mastery of matter and may be inclined to say that all is material, and nothing counts unless you can perceive it with your senses and measure it, there comes a new set of facts outside the range of what used to be thought the domain of science. If anything of the kind happens to ourselves or our friends, let us receive it reverently and not make fun of it. Perhaps God is opening a new window of wonder for men to look through.

Did I say *new*? Why, it is one of the oldest things in the world! When a flock of birds takes flight because one bird on the edge of the flock suspects danger, it is not because any order has gone out. The idea of danger is conveyed by means other than the senses. As animals have these powers, so did early man, probably far more developed than in us to-day. The Bible is full of psychic events. For example, the prophet Elisha knows the counsel privately given to the king of Syria (2 Kings 6. 12). Which is more likely—that Elisha had an elaborate secret service or that he got the knowledge by telepathy? Again, Jesus tells the nobleman of Capernaum who has come to see him at Cana that his son will live. When the father get home he learns that "yesterday at the seventh hour the fever left him", the exact time at which he had received the assurance. Jesus and the sick boy were in touch with each other at a distance (John 4. 46-54). God's only Son realized the will of the heavenly Father, which was hidden from the others. Many things in the Bible which taken literally seemed impossible are coming to be regarded as simple statements of these hidden powers of men.

31

The Resurrection of a Nation

Come from the four winds, O breath, and breathe upon these slain that they may live. EZEKIEL 37. 9.

JERUSALEM AND Judaea are in a state of misery and dejection. A few thousands of the Jews, including the King and the leading men—nobles, priests, and prophets, are exiles in Babylonia bewailing their lot. But thanks to the inspiring faith of one man, Ezekiel, they have never despaired.

He was a man of many visions, the most famous of which is that of the valley of dry bones. Unburied bones to a Jewish ear sounded scandalous, for honourable burial was the right of everyone. That a corpse should lie in the fields, the flesh being plucked away by scavenger birds till nothing but the skeleton was left, was the greatest possible indignity. So the vision emphasized what was the most poignant sorrow to the pious Jew, that he was far from the Holy Land, living in a state of uncleanness and unable to keep the laws of purity. And this no doubt was in Ezekiel's mind; the vision painted in the most vivid way the abyss of wretchedness from which Israel was to be rescued.

In the vision he saw a miracle performed. There was a noise, an earthquake, and then the clashing of the scattered bones as the skeletons were reassembled. But putting together the skeletons was only the first stage. The flesh had to be laid on the bones, and the sinews and muscles added to hold everything together. The body was now formed, but something else was needed, namely life. Now the presence of life is shown by the rhythmical moving of the breath in and out of the body; the breath is simply air in motion. And, for Ezekiel's mind, if breath is to be produced in a lifeless body, it must first come in from outside. Needless to say, he has no idea that the pure air breathed in and the used air, largely carbon dioxide, expelled are different chemically. All is one to him—the breath from the lungs, the air inhaled, and the wind which seems to bring the air from afar. Indeed, there is only one word in Hebrew which is here translated wind,, breath, or spirit.

Ezekiel is not thinking of resurrection of an individual after death but of the corporate resurrection of a dead nation. The way in which he teaches this lesson deserves close study. He is thinking of the creation of man in Genesis, chapter 2, where God forms man of the dust of the ground and then breathes life into him. What Israel now needs is a new creation, a fresh start, power to begin again with all the vigour of youth. The process will be as startling and miraculous as the creation of the first man.

The prophet is not thinking of Israel as becoming a great nation, or even a small one, able to hold its own in the conflicts of the Near East, but rather of a people set free to serve God. Nothing less than a supernatural act on the part of God will be of any use. Israel will live again, but only by the Spirit and in the strength of God.

Modern history provides many illustrations of nations beaten down to the ground by war and rising again by hard work and tenacity of purpose. But we can hardly take them as examples to-day of what Ezekiel prophesied long ago. Rather we must think of the Church, sometimes despised and rejected of men, sometimes sinking into the depths of formalism and sloth, but always having the power of revival. Often through the centuries have good men looked at the Church and asked, "Can these dry bones live?" and always in time the answer Yes has come and an awakening to new life has followed. The Church, like all living organisms, has its periods of sickness and health, but unlike them has indestructible life and will last until the end of the world.

"If any man be in Christ", says St Paul (2 Cor. 5. 17), "he is a new creation", by virtue of his membership in the sacred Body of Christ. The Bible knows nothing of a solitary religion. The individual is not expected to maintain spiritual life without the help of others. All the time he is supported by his brothers and sisters in the faith, while he in his turn gives them help and encouragement. The old Jews have much to teach us, for they always thought in terms of Israel. Israel with its memories of the patriarchs, its experience of God's mighty works, its hopes of a glorious future, its power of patient endurance of present misfortunes, came first to the Jew. The component parts of Israel found life meaningful in so far as they realized that they were parts of a great and inspiring whole.

32

Keep Yourselves from Idols

Keep yourselves from idols. 1 JOHN 5. 21.

THE AUTHOR of the second part of Isaiah, chapters 40 to 55, lived in Babylon and wrote just before and just after the capture of the city by Cyrus in 538. In majestic language he expresses the splendour of the God of Israel, Creator of all things including the stars, which the Babylonians identified with the gods. Then he turns to the practical religion all around him, which was entirely bound up with idols.

Some people might say that idols were a necessary concession to the needs of simple people, what school teachers call "visual aids"; something like a crucifix, which arouses holy thoughts of what the salvation of man cost and therefore to be treated with reverence. But that would be modernizing too much. Idols were treated very seriously. The old records describe how they were provided with comfortable beds, given two main meals a day and two little ones (excellent food, ultimately eaten by the priests), and even taken for drives. The fact is that they were supposed to be impregnated with divine essence and for practical purposes to be the gods they represented.

The prophet, whom we will call Isaiah, was familiar with all this, and we may suppose that some of the Jews in exile were attracted by it, as they had been in their home land. The excuse would be that Babylon had proved itself stronger than Judah and therefore the gods of Babylon were stronger than their God—at least it would be advisable to keep on good terms with them.

Faced by such a situation Isaiah does not argue, he simply resorts to ridicule. He pictures the blacksmith's shop and brass or iron molten in the furnace; or the carpenter's shop. First a tree is cut down and brought into the city. It is large enough to be used for several purposes. With part he makes a fire and bakes bread or roasts meat. If it is a cold winter's day he warms himself in front of the fire and says, "Aha! I am warm". Then with what is left he sets to and makes—a god! What next? He falls down and worships it (Isa. 44).

We may be glad that he was brave enough to tell the truth and did not say, "Well, we must be broad-minded". Some abuses are best met by making fun of them, or at any rate by frontal attack. If after this any Jews had a hankering after idols, it would be with a bad conscience. We have an example of an old bad practice lingering on in the middle of the second century before Christ. Judas Maccabaeus led his army against the enemy and suffered defeat. Dead bodies were picked up and under the clothes were found images. Perhaps they did not mean more than mascots of St Christopher carried by unbelieving motorists; but at least public opinion prevented the Jews from wearing them openly (see 2 Macc. 12. 40).

St Paul at Corinth had to deal with Gentile converts, who had come from surroundings like those at Babylon. What were they to do if they were offered meat which had been killed in honour of a god? (1 Cor. 8. 4). An idol is nothing at all he says; a piece of wood or stone, nothing more. If you are clear in your mind about this, then eat with a good conscience, for you cannot be defiled by nothing. But there are many weak Christians, who cannot get away from the thought that there is something after all in the old religion. They will follow your example, but for them it will mean going back to heathenism. So put the soul of your brother first and, if there is any danger of harming his faith, have nothing to do with food which has a dubious history.

Later, St John ends his first Epistle with: "Little children, keep yourselves from idols" (1 John 5. 21). It is difficult to think that his readers were tempted that way. So he is probably thinking of life in a heathen city, where idols and customs connected with them were universal, and he means play for safety, avoid mixing in heathen social life, it is too dangerous.

The world changes, and there is no fear now of idolatry in the literal sense. But now as much as ever people make false gods for themselves. So many demands of the world have to be conceded, so many luxuries are regarded as necessities and have to be obtained before we give time and money to the worship and service of God, that keeping ourselves from idols will never be out of date.

33

The Servant of the Lord

He was numbered with the transgressors: yet he bare the sin of many, and made intercession for the transgressors.

ISAIAH 53. 12.

CHAPTERS 40 to 55 of Isaiah form a separate part of the book; they were written when Cyrus king of Persia was approaching Babylon and the exiled Jews there were filled with hope of deliverance, or a little later, when the Babylonian empire had fallen and Cyrus had given them permission to go home. But within these chapters are four passages which tell so wonderful a story of one who was to be a missionary of salvation that they can be read together as a connected narrative.

The first passage comes in chapter 42 (verses 1-4). God speaks of his servant, whom he has chosen to be a missionary to the Gentiles. He will use tender and lenient methods, not crying aloud in the streets, and will be very tender to weak souls. "A bruised reed shall he not break, and the smoking flax shall he not quench." In spite of setbacks he will not fail nor be discouraged.

The second passage is found in chapter 49 (verses 1-6), where the servant speaks. He tells of his call from birth. He was kept like an arrow in the quiver until the time came for his mission to begin. Then the Lord discharged the arrow, and the prophet was sent to preach to his own people Israel.

Finally came the call to a wider mission. He had failed, but all the time was being prepared for a grander work. "It is too light a thing that thou shouldest be my servant to raise up the tribes of Jacob, and to restore the preserved of Israel: I will also give thee for a light to the Gentiles, that thou mayest be my salvation unto the end of the earth."

Next comes chapter 50 (verses 4-9), in which the servant describes his experiences. He has had continual inspiration, every morning opening his ears to the word of God. But his preaching has led to persecution. "I give my back to the smiters . . . I hid not my face from shame and spitting." But he still trusts in God. "I set my face like a flint . . . Behold, the Lord God will help me."

The story reaches its climax in chapters 52 (verses 13-15) and 53. God speaks first. "My servant . . . shall be exalted and lifted up." Just as men were astonished at him and his sufferings, so now they will be startled and struck dumb. Then the Gentiles take up the story. Here was a poor persecuted man. "He was despised, and rejected of men; a man of sorrows, and acquainted with grief." Indeed so repellent was he that he was "as one from whom men hide their face", which seems to mean a leper. After he was martyred, we realized that his sufferings were not a punishment inflicted by God. On the contrary, "he was wounded for our transgressions, he was bruised for our iniquities . . . and with his stripes we are healed". They go on to tell how he was put to death, led as an innocent lamb to the slaughter. Then God speaks again. The servant will rise from the dead and prolong his days. He will resume his mission and justify mankind, "because he poured out his soul unto death, and was numbered with the transgressors: yet he bare the sin of many, and made intercession for the transgressors".

Who was this strange man, who strove to divert the Jews from thinking only of themselves, was rejected by them, and went on a mission to the Gentiles, which ended in a martyr's death, and in the end of the story was raised by God from the dead? It is difficult, perhaps impossible, to think of all this as a literal record of historic fact. How would a Jew in Babylon start a mission to the heathen? So far as we know, the idea that the national religion of Israel was meant for the whole world was not formed in the minds of the Jews at this period. Indeed, the other parts of these Isaiah chapters show that they rejected it. Thus we have "Who is blind but my servant? or deaf as my messenger that I send?" (42. 19). Unlike the servant we have been studying, the servant here is Israel, blind to the wonderful new prospect, deaf to the new call.

Then who is the servant in these passages? I see no possible answer except the old one, that it is Jesus Christ. The prophet is trying to understand a wonderful revelation of God's purpose. He sees a vision of a perfectly good man, who lays down his life for his fellow men and is raised from the dead by the righteous and loving Father. Inevitably he expresses his conviction in veiled words, using the ideas and language of his day; that the servant could only be the Son of God he could not know. But through the veil the Cross shines through.

Christ himself used the prophesy to describe his mission. He was chary of using the word Christ, which was liable to be misunderstood. He was indeed an anointed king, but a king of a new kind, giving his life "as a ransom for many", his blood "for you and for many for the remission of sins".

34

Church and State

There are the two anointed ones, that stand by the Lord of the whole earth. ZECHARIAH 4. 14.

WHEN THE exiled Jews returned to Jerusalem, Cyrus the Persian king made a great concession. Instead of appointing a Persian as governor, he gave the post to a native Jew. However for eighteen years nothing much happened; indeed, as we learn from Haggai, the temple was not built.

But in 520 B.C. the curtain goes up and for a few months we are able to follow the hopes and disappointments of the Jews in the pages of two prophets, Haggai and Zechariah. The first governor seems to have died, and was succeeded by Zerubbabel, who was not only a Jew but of the royal line of David, being grandson of King Jehoiachin who had been taken into exile 77 years before. The hopes of the Jews rose high, encouraged by political events. The new Persian king, Darius, succeeded to the throne two years earlier, but his succession was disputed and he had to fight in order to secure it. The Jews hoped that the Messianic Kingdom would be set up with Zerubbabel as its prince. We learn from Haggai (2. 23) that he was regarded as the signet-ring on the hand of the Lord, which means that he had divine authority, was God's prime minister so to speak, and his orders were to be regarded as executing the will of God.

But the new age was precious in the eyes of the Jews because they would be free to practise their religion. So the religious head of the people, Joshua the high priest, was regarded as equal to the Governor. Together they worked at their first and most important task, the rebuilding of the Temple. How could God's kingdom be expected to come if God's house had not been built?

This double method of ruling is described by Zechariah in picture language. He sees the candelabra used in the temple services with its bowls filled with oil. On each side stands an olive tree, from which the oil flows in pipes to supply the candelabra. Zechariah asks what the vision means and receives this explanation: "These are the two anointed ones, that stand by the Lord of the whole earth." They are the civil and religious leaders of the nation. They are equal in authority; both are consecrated for their work and both have their links with heaven, for they "stand by the Lord of the whole earth".

This was a unique experience. Apparently it lasted for a very short time, and then Zerubbabel disappeared from history, being replaced by a Persian governor. Then the high priest became very important. He was the Jews' own man and stood for their religious ideals. Only then did the title "high priest" come into general use; we might almost say that he took the place of the old kings.

Short-lived as the experiment was, it is full of teaching for later times. Knowing what human nature is like, we suspect that the experiment would have failed before long, but for a short time it was successful. The story remains as a splendid ideal of Church and State, not rivals but partners. As we look back on history we see how uneasy the partnership has always been. The State has put worldly things first and has often found the Church's insistence on religion and morals a nuisance. The Church has found the yoke of the State burdensome and has been tempted to regard it as a hindrance to religion. But a strong State is necessary if the Church is to do its work. Where should we be without a police force to maintain order and punish crime? "Order is heaven's first law." In the modern Welfare State much of the social work once done by the Church has passed under the control of the State, which is, or may be, a power for good. If the State is secular, it is also to a large extent post-*Christian*, still permeated to a large extent by the ideals of Christianity. Obedience to the "powers that be", which are "ordained by God", is taught by St Paul (Rom. 13. 1). Though the personal representative of power was Nero, he could yet say this. St Peter, who was to suffer a cruel death under Nero, used similar language: "Be subject to every ordinance of man for the Lord's sake: whether it be to the kings, as supreme; or unto governors, as sent by him . . ." (1 Pet. 2. 13). Those who live under a monarchy which for so long has set an example of public service and adherence to the Christian faith, and is hallowed by the solemn rite of Coronation, have far more reason than the first hearers of the Apostles to accept their teaching. But the old order of words, Church and State, the Church coming first, remains. In the last resort we must put the Church first and obey God rather than men.

35

A Tract for Bad Times

They that feared the Lord spake one with another.
MALACHI 3. 16.

BOOKS HAVE been published with titles like "From Malachi to Matthew", the idea being that the Old Testament ends with Malachi and the New Testament begins with Matthew. But this is too simple a way of expressing it. Malachi happens to be the last book of the Old Testament in the English Bible, but in the Hebrew it comes not far after the middle. Quite a number of books were written after Malachi, to say nothing of the Apocrypha.

Malachi was written nearly 500 years before Christ, when the little State of Judah was going through a bad time. The first vigour of the return from exile, which produced the re-building of the Temple, had died down, and the Jews formed a depressed, poverty-stricken little community, up to a point managing their own affairs but under a Persian governor and paying taxes to their foreign lords. They had grown slack in their religion, about which they said, so Malachi tells us (1. 13), "What a weariness it is!" Then God raised up a prophet to rebuke them and stir them to take religion seriously. We do not know his name. "Malachi" means "my messenger" and is taken from a verse of the book, "Behold, I send my messenger" (3. 1).

The first chapter deals with the laity and their slackness, especially as regards outward observances, of which sacrifice was the most important. A bad habit had grown up of choosing a worthless beast, blind or lame, to be offered to God. In itself that may seem to us not very serious, but it showed a deplorable state of mind. As the prophet says, Try it on the Governor! You would not dare to do such a thing. You have enough belief in God not to give up religion but you think any old thing will do for God. Look at the piety of the Gentiles: "In every place incense is offered in my name, and a pure offering" (1. 11). This seems to mean that the Gentiles in worshipping their own gods are really worshipping the one true God; it is the best they can do, so long as they are ignorant of him.

Then Malachi turns to the priests. They have neglected an important part of their duty. "The priest's lips should keep knowledge." This does not refer to the niceties of theology but to practical directions on the problems of every-day life.

Priests and laity alike must look forward to the Day of Judgement, when the Lord whom they seek will suddenly come to his Temple. His action is compared to that of a refiner of silver, who melts the metal in the fire and purges out the base elements, leaving nothing but pure silver. The curious feature of this prophecy is that there is no mention of a Messiah; the Lord comes in person. And it is not in any sense the end of the world. "Then shall the offering of Judah and Jerusalem be pleasant unto the Lord, as in the days of old" (3. 4). Life goes on as before but in a more worthy way. Meanwhile, pending the arrival of that day, a messenger will be sent—"my messenger", who "shall prepare the way before me". Later (4. 5) he is described as "Elijah the prophet". In what sense this is meant we cannot be sure; it may mean a succession of prophets. In the Gospels John the Baptist is called Elijah, since he does the work which Elijah had done long ago.

Meanwhile what are God's people to do? Two remarkable verses give the answer (3. 16, 17). "They that feared the Lord spake one with another." The godly few gather together in a kind of group or cell for prayer and mutual help. "And the Lord hearkened . . . and a book of remembrance was written before him for them that feared the Lord, and that thought upon his name." Why this is remarkable needs to be explained. The idea had always been that Israel was a holy people, and that God kept a register in which all names were written down. There was no test, to belong to the holy people was sufficient qualification. But now the book is for the godly few in Israel. It is to them that the lovely promise is made: "They shall be mine in the day that I act, even a peculiar people"; or in the better known words of the Authorized Version, "in that day when I make up my jewels". So here we have Bible authority for prayer groups within the congregation, small groups of like-minded people who meet to help each other in the spiritual life. Such groups can do nothing but good, provide they put away any thought of being superior to the rest who prefer not to join them.

36

For all Nations

My house shall be called a house of prayer for all nations.

ISAIAH 56. 7.

THE LAST eleven chapters of Isaiah are concerned with the situation in Judah after the exiles came back from Babylon and had built the Temple, roughly speaking with the years between 500 and 450 B.C. They are a curious mixture; some passages display lofty spirituality, others a narrow religion that is in danger of self-satisfaction. Everything was in a state of flux, and nobody knew how things would turn out.

The Jews had not yet made up their minds about the other inhabitants of Palestine. Far the larger part of the land was the old northern kingdom, now called Samaria, which for some 250 years had been under foreign rule and had no strong religious leaders. No wonder abuses had crept in. While the population was predominantly Hebrew, there had been a considerable immigration of foreigners, from Babylonia and the countries next to Israel. These had tried to worship God (2 Kings 17. 26) but had never been really "converted", as we might say. So the last chapters of Israel tell of many heathen practices, which horrified strict Jews.

Now there were two possible policies. The first was to welcome everyone into the fold. To our minds this sounds the liberal and wise method. The danger was that true religion would be swamped by an infiux of uninstructed people. The second policy was for the Jews to withdraw into their shell, make the laws stricter, keep strangers out, and try to be God's holy people. This was the policy that prevailed, and we cannot doubt that it was justified in view of the prevailing conditions. Narrow-minded as it seems to us, it at least gave the Jews a breathing-space in which to develop their own way of life.

Let us consider what the programme of the Broad Church party really meant. In the days of the Exile a great man arose, whose message is found in chapters 40 to 55 of Isiah. He told of the Servant of the Lord, who was called to be a missionary to the Gentiles and suffered martyrdom, apparently at the hands of his own people. He is an isolated figure; except for Jonah, who is sent to Ninevah as an unwilling preacher of salvation, there is nothing like him elsewhere in the Old Testament. But, if the Jews at this time did not go to the Gentiles, they had no objection to the Gentiles coming to them. Indeed there is a good deal about this in the last chapters of Isaiah. The wealth of the nations will flow in to Judah—on camels from Arabia, in ships from the Mediterranean lands. The walls of Jerusalem will be built—by foreigners, who will do servile work for the Jews. The gates of the city will be open day and night to admit the tribute. "That nation and kingdom that will not serve thee shall perish" (60. 6-12). "Strangers shall stand and feed thy flocks, and aliens shall be your plowmen and your vine-dressers" (61. 5), The prophet goes on to say: "Ye shall be named the priests of the Lord . . . ye shall eat the wealth of the nations" (61. 6).

We see now what he is driving at. Israel is to be the priestly nation; as the laity in Israel support the priests, so the Gentiles will support Israel. Jerusalem is to be the spiritual metropolis of the world. The court of the Temple is to be open to all people, "a house of prayer for all nations". who, however, are expected to accept permanent inferiority.

Turn to the New Testament and think of Jesus cleansing the Temple, turning out the money-changers and saying: "Is it not written, my house shall be called a house of prayer for all the nations, but ye have made it a den of thieves?" (Mark 11. 17). This is in St Mark. St Matthew in telling the

story leaves out the important words "for all the nations".
Jesus is in the outer court of the Temple, known as the Court
of the Gentiles. It was not holy if open to Gentiles, and so
any kind of trading could take place there. But Jesus claims
the whole building for God's house. His mission was to Israel
first, and only on rare occasions could he give attention to
Gentiles. But by this act he defined what was to be the true
attitude to foreigners in the coming Kingdom of God; and
his great follower St Paul carried out the purpose of his master by preaching that in Christ the distinction between Jew
and Gentile has come to an end.

37

The Mission of Jonah

Arise, go to Nineveh, that great city, and cry against it.
JONAH 1. 2.

IT IS sad that a lovely book like Jonah, which gives so full
an assurance of God's mercy and love, should be familiar to
most people only from the incident of the whale, which
naturally strikes us as comic; or from the dropping out of a
team as a "Jonah" some man who seems to bring bad luck.
The writer has a message to deliver, nothing less than that
salvation is offered to the whole world, even to the most
cruel foes of Israel. With the perfection of artistic skill he
puts his message in the form of a story. Now there was one
period in Jewish history when the attitude to be adopted
towards the Gentiles was a subject of lively debate, the fifth
century before Christ, when under the guidance of Ezra and
Nehemiah Judaism closed its ranks, shut out the Gentiles,
and even made Jews who had married foreign wives put them

away. The book of Ruth pleads for a more sympathetic attitude towards foreigners, and so does Jonah in its way. Let us see how it pleads the cause of the Gentiles.

The call comes to Jonah to go and preach to Nineveh. Jonah stands for Israel, which indeed has the true faith, but has it in order to share it with others. He refuses the call and tries to flee from the Lord by taking a ship to Tarshish. The Jews were not sailors, and he would use a ship belonging to the Phoenicians, who had planted colonies as far away as Spain. He could not escape; the God of the Hebrews has jurisdiction outside the Holy Land and sends a storm. The sailors, pagans though they are, are religious and pray to their own gods; Jonah is down below asleep and has to be woken up and told to pray. They, who are in a sense converted, and he agree that the God of Israel has sent the storm to punish Jonah's disobedience, and reluctantly the sailors accept his offer to be thrown overboard; whereupon the storm ceases.

Now comes the great fish. Whether it is a whale or a shark need not be discussed, for it is not meant to be taken literally. The Bible tells us this plainly in Jeremiah, chapter 51 (verses 34, 44). Israel is speaking—"Nebuchadnezzar hath devoured me . . . he hath swallowed me up like a dragon . . . he hath cast me out . . . I will bring forth out of his mouth that which he hath swallowed up." The language, then, is a vivid pictorial way of describing the exile. Israel as a nation is swallowed up by Babylon and after a time is released from captivity. Here we get the clue to the story of Jonah. It is not meant to be history, rather divine teaching in the form of a story.

Then God calls Jonah again: Go and preach to Nineveh. Israel after the Exile has a second chance of fulfilling its destiny and preaching salvation to the heathen world. This time Jonah reluctantly obeys and proclaims God's judgement on Nineveh. A miracle! Nineveh repents and the threat to destroy the wicked city is withdrawn. From what follows we learn how completely the Jews have got their scale of values wrong. Jonah is disgusted. He has come all this way for nothing. "Was not this my saying, when I was yet in my country?" I knew that you would relent and not destroy Nineveh after all. You've made me look such a fool.

However, Jonah does not give up hope. He goes out of the city and finds a place where he can have a good view of the destruction of Nineveh. It is very hot, but a gourd springs up overnight and provides welcome shade. He waits all day, and nothing happens. Next day he takes up his position again, finds that the gourd has withered away, and loses his temper. "Let me die rather than put up with this!" Then God gently rebukes him. "You had pity on the gourd, for which you had done nothing. Think of me. I made all the inhabitants of Nineveh. Of course I have compassion and long for them to repent. Why! there are 120,000 little children who do not yet know the difference between the right hand and the left. To say nothing of the dumb animals, which also I made. Do you think I want to destroy my creatures?" And so the story ends with the picture of God's mercy brooding over the great heathen city.

Is there any lesson more needed to-day, when the countries of the West are pressing forward to an ever higher standard of living and the good things of the world are so unequally divided between the haves and the have-nots? Long before there was any clear picture in men's minds of the divine Saviour of the world, loving men enough to die for them, this unknown Hebrew writer had a vision of God's all-embracing love for those he had made. The message was not heeded. Judaism adopted a policy of intolerance, excluding Gentiles and refusing co-operation with them. Probably it was inevitable, for otherwise they might have been swamped by heathen influences. But, although Jonah's teaching was not accepted, the book was included in the Bible and remained as a witness to God's purpose for mankind, a part of the Gospel embedded in the Old Testament.

38

The Story of Ruth

Thy people shall be my people, and thy God my God. . . .
A full reward shall be given thee of the Lord, the God of
Israel, under whose wings thou art come to take refuge.
RUTH 1. 16; 2. 12.

BY PUTTING Ruth after Judges the English Bible suggests that it has that grim and savage book as its background. But in the Hebrew Bible Ruth comes near the end among the later books of the Old Testament, and scholars are agreed in following this lead. We conclude that it is a story, whether founded on fact or not does not matter; in reality a very short novel. The Old Testament contains histories, lawbooks, manuals of ethics, hymns, love-songs—why not novels or stories? Our Lord himself has set the seal of his approval on stories by such parables as the Prodigal Son and the Good Samaritan.

The interest of the book of Ruth is greatly increased when we know the real background. In the fifth century before Christ a great debate was taking place in Judah. How should the Jews treat the Gentiles? The books of Ezra and Nehemiah tell us how it was decided. One party said, Let the Temple be a house of prayer for all nations; let us be missionary hearted and welcome proselytes. The other said, Let us close our ranks; we can't afford to be liberal and dilute the wine of pure religion. All kinds of heathen corruptions will come in. To be on the safe side—and this is what Ezra succeeded in doing—let us make Jews who have married foreigners put away their wives. They found a passage in the law of Moses which said that "a Moabite shall not enter into the assembly of God for ever" (Neh. 13. 1; Deut. 23. 3-5), and acted upon it. As so often in history, each side had a good case, but perhaps the intolerant line, which does not appeal to us, was right then.

The author of Ruth boldly said, I will write a book in which the heroine, the ideal proselyte, the most charming and virtuous woman I can imagine, is a Moabite.

You know the story. Naomi, her husband, and her two sons, leave Bethlehem in a famine and go to live in Moab. The husband dies, and his two sons, and Naomi is left with Orpah and Ruth, the Moabite girls whom her sons have married. Both want to go to Bethlehem with her. She dissuades Orpah, but Ruth insists on going, uttering the immortal words: "Where thou goest, I will go . . . Thy people shall be my people, and thy God my God . . . naught but death shall part thee and me." She is prepared to change nationality and religion rather than desert Naomi.

The women reach Bethlehem at the beginning of harvest and Ruth gleans in the field of Boaz, a well-to-do farmer. The story now becomes rather puzzling until we understand the social customs of the time. If a man died childless, his brother, or the next of kin if there was no brother, had to act as a husband to her. There was no suggestion of lust. Indeed, the duty was often distasteful. If a child was born, it was not his but by a legal fiction the child of the dead brother, and the property that should have come to him reverted to the other branch of the family. With matchless purity and simplicity the story tells how Ruth made herself known to Boaz and reminded him of the obligation. We cannot help wondering whether in real life there ever was such a harvest scene as that which depicts the farmer greeting the labourers with, "The Lord be with you", and the labourers answering, "The Lord bless thee". Legal form had to be observed. Boaz was not the brother of Ruth's deceased husband, and another man was a nearer kinsman. So a primitive Court was held at the city gate. The other man was told that it was his duty to redeem the land that had belonged to Naomi's husband in order to keep it in the family, and to take Ruth. This meant parting with his money and, if a child was born, not getting the land. So he abdicated in favour of Boaz, and all ended happily. A baby boy came and was named Obed. He was the father of Jesse, and Jesse the father of David.

The sting is in the tail. You, so the author means, and no one could miss the point, are driving out foreign wives even if they are devout worshippers of your God. You have a special animus against the Moabites. But long ago a Moabite woman came to Bethlehem, an example of the perfect proselyte, and she became the mother of a boy who grew up to be the grandfather of your great King David

39

The Coming of the Law

The joy of the Lord is your strength. NEHEMIAH 8. 10.

THIS CHAPTER of Nehemiah is one of the most dramatic in the Old Testament. It describes how Ezra the priest brought the Law from Babylonia to the Jews, long after the return from exile, and imposed it on the people, with the backing of the Persian King. Ezra is one of the key-men of the Bible, being the founder of Judaism as we know it to-day. The days of the great prophets were over, and what mattered now was "the Jewish way of life", consisting in strict obedience to the

Law. The rapt attention of the people as they heard him read the Law shows that it was largely new to them; we must suppose that the learned Jews of Babylonia had produced a new edition of the Law of Moses, brought up to date in the light of modern problems.

We must remember that by this time the ordinary man or woman in Judah no longer understood Hebrew; the Persians had made Aramaic, a kindred tongue, the official language of the western part of their empire. This explains the procedure followed on the historic day. Ezra had a wooden pulpit or platform made. He stood on this above the people, with his helpers on each side. He read the Law in Hebrew, and they translated it into Aramaic, with an interpretation. This means that, if the meaning was not perfectly clear, they expanded the sentences in order to explain them. The congregation had been accustomed to take things from the priests on trust; now for the first time they understood the sacred document. "The people . . . made great mirth, because they understood the words that were declared unto them."

It was indeed an historic occasion. On that day was formed the pattern of Jewish worship in the synagogue—reading the Bible, explaining it in a sermon, praise, and prayer. As we all know, this is the pattern of our Church services other than Holy Communion. When our Lord went to the synagogue of Nazareth, he was handed the Bible, from which he read a passage and then gave its meaning for the present generation (Luke 4). He made a tremendous impression, not indeed favourable, for the Rabbis did not dare to give their own explanation but merely repeated that handed down from the past.

This, then, was the beginning of Judaism as a complete written system of law. To our minds it sounds cramping, certainly not inspiring. But the Jews did not feel like that. At first they wept, realizing how far their practice fell below the precepts of the Law. But Ezra told them not to weep. "This day is holy unto our Lord . . . the joy of the Lord is your strength."

It was a wonderful thing, to know what was God's will for them and to feel that they could please him by careful observance of every detail of the holy book. Psalm 119 shows us the mind of a devout Jew. It is all one long hymn of praise of the Law. "Oh, how I love thy Law", is the refrain, repeated constantly in slightly different ways. It rings the changes on the various words for the Law. Thus in the first eight verses we find "way", "testimonies", "precepts", "statutes", "commandments", "judgements". There was no attempt to discriminate between the different items of the Law. "Thou shalt love thy neighbour as thyself" and "Thou shalt not seethe a kid in its mother's milk" were both important as examples of God's will for his people.

Clearly this idea of the Law could not be permanent. The Law was intended to discipline and train God's people—but to train them for what? Surely for one who could speak with personal authority. "It was said to them of old time . . . *but I say unto you* . . ." The tragedy was that, when the Son of God came and declared God's will, the Jews trained in the Law rejected him as an impostor.

40

The Coming of the Spirit

> I will pour out my spirit upon all flesh; and your sons and your daughters shall prophesy, your old men shall dream dreams, your young men shall see visions; and also upon the servants and upon the handmaids in those days will I pour out my spirit. JOEL 2. 28, 29.

THE TEACHING of the Church about the Holy Spirit is an essential part of our religion. We believe that Jesus is the

Son of God, that he died for our salvation, and rose again. But after all he is a figure in history, a history of long ago that recedes rapidly from our gaze in this tempestuous modern world. The doctrine of the Spirit teaches us that all we need, both of the Father and the Son, is with us now in the Spirit. And the Spirit is the infinite God; in no way are we handicapped in comparison with the original disciples. We have Christ when we have the Spirit. Recall Christ's words in St John's Gospel: "I will pray the Father, and he shall give you another Comforter, that he may be with you for ever . . . I will not leave you comfortless; I will come unto you" (14. 16, 18). The Spirit is Christ, invisible indeed, but with us for ever.

How did all this begin? We expect to find anticipations of Christian teaching in the Old Testament, but it may be a surprise to realize how few they are in this case. God's people were in the Infants' School and had to begin with elementary things.

In Judges we read of Samson encountering a lion. The spirit of the Lord came upon him, and he tore the lion to pieces with his bare hands (14. 6). Again, strengthened by the spirit, he killed a thousand Philistines with the jawbone of an ass (15. 15). An impulse of strength came to him from outside, and he was able to do marvellous things. Nowadays we should describe this as a psychological rather than religious event. Again, we read that Saul, having been anointed by Samuel as king, meets a band of prophets, who play on instruments and inspire him to become a new man; this is described as "the spirit of the Lord" coming on Saul (1 Sam. 10. 6, 10). In a more religious way, the spirit of the Lord seizes Ezekiel and moves him from one place to another, to do God's bidding. It is curious that the inspiration of the prophets, which we should expect to come through the Holy Spirit, is generally described by phrases like "the word of the Lord came" to Jeremiah, etc.

Twice only in the Old Testament does the phrase "*holy spirit*" occur. Once in Psalm 51, "take not thy holy spirit from me", a prayer which comes in Mattins and Evensong. The other place is Isaiah 63, where it is said that Israel grieved God's holy spirit; and, immediately afterwards, that God "put his holy spirit in the midst of them". We see the beginnings of a much deeper idea of the Spirit, which is *holy*, different from all other possible spirits, good or bad, being the Spirit of the one holy God.

However, when we come to our text, we find a new and wonderful vision of the future. "I will pour out my spirit upon all flesh. And your sons and daughters shall prophesy, your old men shall dream dreams, your young men shall see visions; and also upon the servants and upon the handmaids in those days will I pour out my spirit." This is a prophecy of the last days, when God will bring in the New Age. The novelty to the Jews who first heard it would be that the promise applied to everyone. Hitherto the general idea of the Spirit had been that it was an endowment reserved for kings and heroes, figures of national importance. Now the outpouring was to be upon all, even slaves. So far the Spirit had come on great men for a special purpose and was liable to be withdrawn. Now, in the Messianic Age, when God would intervene to save his people, it would be the permanent possession of all.

Apart from these few passages, little was said about the Spirit until Christ came. John the Baptist said, "I baptized you with water, but he shall baptize you with the Holy Ghost" (Mark 1. 8). In other words, the times of the Messiah were at hand, and would be marked by the coming of the Holy Spirit; all citizens of the Kingdom would receive the Spirit. At Pentecost the promise came true, and the believers found more than a spiritual gift—the very presence of their Lord and Saviour.

41

Job and the Problem of Suffering (i)

Ye have heard of the patience of Job. JAMES 5. 11.

FOR MANY people to-day the main religious problem is, Why should I suffer? They would probably be surprised to learn that in the Bible the corresponding problem is, Why do men sin and rebel against God? Whereas most of us think of a rising standard of living for ourselves and our families and feel a grievance if we are deprived of it, the people of the Bible took disaster and suffering as part of man's lot on earth; prosperity was God's reward for pleasing him, adversity the necessary punishment for sin. In the New Testament St Paul goes deeply into the problems involved by sin and suffering. In the Old Testament only one writer, the man who wrote Job, seems to have been seriously troubled by them. Let us study his contribution to the discussion.

We must distinguished between the first two and the last chapters, which are written in prose, on the one hand, and the rest of the book, which is all poetry, on the other. There is a great difference between them. The prose story tells of a famous man who suffered unjustly and bore his troubles with wonderful patience; he is referred to by St James ("Ye have heard of the patience of Job"). But the Job of the poem is most impatient, complaining about his misfortunes and doubting the justice of God. The prose story illustrates popular Hebrew piety and may be very old. The poems show us the thinking of a master-mind grappling with deep thoughts. The profound discussions are put in the framework of the well-known tale, which ends happily with Job once more prosperous. Without this conventional happy ending the body of the book might never have been accepted as an inspired contribution to the Bible. The fall of Jerusalem and the banishment of the Jewish leaders to Babylon broke down the old optimism of the Hebrews, who had to come to terms with the new situation. What they made of it we shall see.

The prose story of the first two chapters is finely told. It concerns the problem of disinterested goodness: "doth Job serve God for nought?" The opening scene is laid in heaven, where Satan, who acts as public prosecutor, accuses Job; he has gone up and down the world to find pure goodness. Job, for example, is a model of piety, but he has made a good thing out of his religion. It is easy to be good when you are prosperous. Reduce him to poverty and see what happens. Satan is given leave to "tempt" Job, that is to test him; he may deprive him of everything but not touch the man himself. By a succession of blows Job loses his sons and daughters, flocks and herds. This was a terrible trial: first, because the death of his children was to a Hebrew the greatest possible calamity; secondly, because he would take disaster as a proof of God's displeasure. Job with wonderful piety says: "The Lord gave, and the Lord hath taken away; blessed be the name of the Lord."

Satan next reports progress and is permitted to hit Job's person, as hard as he likes so long as life is preserved. Presently we find the poor man smitten apparently with leprosy, banished from his fellow men, and sitting on a rubbish heap outside the village, where he scrapes himself with a broken piece of pottery. His wife nags him—this is what you get for your piety—"renounce God and die". She means, blaspheme God so vigorously that he will smite you dead and end your troubles. Job gives a noble answer; "Thou speakest as one of the foolish women speaketh. What? Shall we receive good at the hand of God, and shall we not receive evil?" By evil he means misfortune, not moral evil. In the thought of the day God *sent* whatever he allowed, there was no idea of secondary causes; Satan is supposed to be still in heaven.

Then the three friends arrive, having heard the bad news.

They sit in grave, sympathetic silence before the sufferer. There is no hint in these chapters that they are to prove voluble, unsympathetic, even merciless, as in the poem that follows.

We pass on to the last chapter. Job is reinstated, his family is exactly replaced, and his property, large enough to begin with, is doubled. This happy ending was necessary. When there was no clear idea of the next life. God's goodness had to be shown in this life. To us the ending seems inartistic, even slightly ludicrous when we read of the new set of daughters— Jemimah, Keziah, and Keren-Happuch. But we have learned valuable lessons, for Job has shown the possibility of disinterested goodness. He has been utterly humble and has made no claims on God, whom he will serve with equal devotion in bad times as well as good. With superb manliness he takes disaster in his stride, making no complaint. The Christian has a fuller light and a conception of suffering denied to Job, but the old hero has given us splendid foundation on which to build.

42

Job and the Problem of Suffering (ii)

I know that my Redeemer liveth. JOB 19. 25.

LAST WEEK we considered the old-world story of Job's sufferings and his restoration to prosperity. We now go on to the poetical part of the book, which is in the form of dialogues, and see how the author grappled with the problem of suffering, without our knowledge of the Cross and with only a shadowy belief in a future life.

Job begins by bemoaning his cruel fate. I didn't ask to be born. If I had to be born, why didn't I die at birth and go to the place where

> the wicked cease from troubling:
> and there the weary are at rest?
>
> (3. 17)

With chapter 4 the speeches of the friends begin. Eliphaz, Bildad and Zophar each make three speeches, which Job answers; at least this was the original plan, but Zophar's third speech is missing. The three friends repeat the same arguments; only Job makes any real progress. Eliphaz speaks first and claims to have had a special revelation.

> Now a thing was secretly brought to me,
> And mine ear received a whisper thereof,
> In thoughts from the visions of the night,
>   when deep sleep falleth on men,
> Fear came upon me, and trembling,
>   which made all my bones to shake.
> Then a spirit passed before my face;
>   the hair of my flesh stood up,
> It stood still, but I could not distinguish
>   the appearance thereof;
>   a form was before my eyes:
>   there was a silence, and I heard a voice,
>   saying,
> Shall man be more just than God?
> Shall a man be more pure than his maker?
>
> (4. 12-17)

We expect something better than this conclusion, with which all would agree. Eliphaz, however, has something to say. He is trying to make it easy for Job to confess that his sins have led to this punishment, which he must accept as just. You can't sit in judgement on God. Be good in future, and all will be well.

> Thou shalt come to thy grave in a full age,
>   like as a shock of corn cometh up in its season.
>
> (5. 26)

Job replies indignantly. I *am* impatient, but with good cause. God will not leave me alone. What harm have I done him?

> What is man, that thou shouldest magnify him,
>   and that thou shouldest set thine heart
>   upon him?
>
>   (7. 17)

meaning, Why dost thou think him worthy of so much attention?

Bildad next suggests that all may yet be well; there are sudden reversals of fortune, the good can be restored to prosperity. Yes, says Job, I know that God can do anything, but *is he righteous*?

> If a man contend with him,
> Can he answer him one of a thousand questions?
>
>   (9. 3)

God holds all the cards, he isn't fair.

> For he is not a man, as I am, that I should
>   answer his summons,
>   that we should come together in judgement.
>
>   (9. 32)

Then, with a sudden resolve, I will face him after all, on one condition.

> Let him take his rod away from me,
>   and let not his terror make me afraid.
>
>   (9. 34)

It might be a frightened child speaking.

Zophar can only repeat the old tale; Put away sin and all will be well. Job is exasperated: "No doubt but ye are the people, and wisdom shall die with you" (12. 2). He goes on to muse:

Man that is born of woman
  is of few days, and full of trouble.
He cometh forth like a flower, and is cut down:
He fleeth also as a shadow, and continueth not.

          (14. 1, 2)

There is no hope for him. "There is hope for a tree, if it is
cut down, that it will sprout again" (14. 7); but "man lieth
down and riseth not: till the heavens be no more, they shall
not awake" (14. 12).

   Then a faint hope dawns. Eventually God may show love
instead of wrath, and meanwhile Job may perhaps be kept
till better times in the shadowy realm of the departed.

    Oh that thou wouldest hide me in Sheol,
       that thou wouldest keep me secret until thy
              wrath is past.

          (14. 13)

But no! "If a man die, shall he live again?" (14. 14.) We
pass on to the best known verses of the book, containing "I
know that my Redeemer liveth", which read somewhat as
follows:

    Why do ye persecute me as God does? . . .
    Oh that my words were now written!
    Oh that they were inscribed in a book!
    That with iron pen and lead
      they were written in the rock for ever!

(I appeal to the verdict of posterity. Even so my case may go
by default.)

    But I know that my Vindicator will live on
      and that he shall stand up in my place upon
            the dust (on my tomb);
    and after my flesh has sunk in decay

Yet apart from my flesh (as a disembodied spirit)
　　shall I see God:
　　whom I shall see to be on my side
(and mine eyes shall behold), and not estranged.

　　　　　　　　　　　　　　　　(19. 22-7)

The word translated "Redeemer" or "Vindicator" is *go-el*, a
Hebrew term for the next-of-kin, whose duty it was to avenge
murder, in days when there were no police. He had other
duties, as we learn from the book of Ruth. When Ruth's
nearest relative refused to fulfil his obligations, Boaz, a more
distant kinsman, took his place and married the foreign girl.
Job makes a tremendous act of faith. God who created him is
his next-of-kin; he at least will live on for ever and see that
justice is done. And Job, though only as a disembodied spirit,
will be allowed to be present at the final vindication. He
appeals from the God of wrath whose anger burns so fiercely
to the God of love who will one day prove to be the true
"next-of-kin". In this wonderful passage we get a glimpse of
the coming belief in a future life. The Hebrews reacted
strongly from everything to do with Egypt, including the
attempt to secure immortality by making mummies of the
dead. Everything of this kind passed away, and their belief in
a future life grew from a new root, which was the nature of
God. God made me, says Job; who else can be my next-of-
kin and vindicator? If vindication now is impossible, then
there must be a life after death, in which God's mercy and
love, clouded over by the troubles of this life, may be mani-
fested. Job stands alone against the religious opinion of his
time and becomes the great pioneer of faith.

43

Job and the Problem of Suffering (iii)

Elihu said . . . Hold thy peace, and I will teach thee wisdom.
JOB 33. 33.

WE HAVE studied the old story of Job, as given in the first
two and the last chapters of the book; and we have also
looked at the poetry, ending with the great text, "I know
that my Redeemer liveth". We pass on to Elihu, whose speech
occupies chapters 32 to 37. He presents the views of
ordinary Judaism, and attacks Job for his impiety and the
three friends for the feebleness of their arguments. He claims
to stand for the younger generation. "I am young, and ye are
very old" (32. 6). The only new point he makes is that suffering is used by God to purify the character. This is true
enough; as Browning says,

> Then, welcome each rebuff
> That turns earth's smoothness rough.

But we soon come to the limits of its truth, for everything
depends on the person. If some are purified by suffering,
others become bitter. Also it is a danger sign when we find
ourselves saying, "It's doing me good". That way lies
priggishness.

The two main questions raised so far are: "Have I
deserved my suffering?" and, "Is it doing me good?" The
wider scope of, "Does my suffering help others?" or, "Is it a
factor in the redemption of the world?" was beyond the
horizon of our author. The great 53rd chapter of Isaiah raises
these issues and points to the answer to all our problems given
by the Cross of Christ; but we cannot expect such an insight
in the ordinary thinkers of the time.

In chapters 38 to 41 of Job we have God's answer, which is impressive but not satisfying. Someone has said: "When you have lost all your property and your children have been killed and you sitting on a dunghill, scraping your scabs with a broken bit of pottery and listening to the nagging of your wife, it is inadequate, to say the least, to be told, 'Look at the hippopotamus'."

Now the references to the hippopotamus and the crocodile form part of a description of the wonders of Nature, much of which is noble and inspiring.

> Where wast thou when I laid the foundations
> of the earth . . .
> When the morning stars sang together,
> And all the sons of God shouted for joy?
>
> (38. 4, 7)

The wonders of the sea, night and day, the rain, the stars, are recounted. There is a charming touch in "cause it to rain on a land where no man is" (38. 26). Do not suppose that everything is done for man's convenience. You were not there when I made things and so cannot understand my purposes. The description of the war-horse is sublime.

> As oft as the trumpet sounds he saith, Aha!
> And he smelleth the battle afar off,
> The thunder of the captains and the shouting.
>
> (39. 25)

Faced with these questions, Job lays down his arms.

> I know that thou canst do all things,
> and that no purpose of thine can be restrained . . .
> Therefore have I uttered that which I understood
> not,
> things too wonderful for me, which I knew not . . .
> I had heard of thee by the hearing of the ear,
> but now mine eye seeth thee,

116

Wherefore I abhor myself, and repent in dust and
                                    ashes.
                             (42. 2-6)

He is content to know that God's ways are not our ways,
and to play a humble part in God's plan of creation.

The modern reader delights in the poetry of this wonderful
book but is left unsatisfied. Who is this all-powerful God that
demands utter submission? He himself looks out on his
fellow-men and, though he recognizes power, finds love the
master-word. To have mercy, to soften the blows of fate
which fall on other men—surely this is what we reverence
most of all. And, if men are made in the image of God, we
may expect that God will, to say the least, not fall short of
men. A God who is merely all-powerful does not command
our love. However, we cannot expect to find the whole of
divine truth in every book of the Bible.

But what a noble book it is, and what important lessons it
teaches! For one thing, it encourages us to use our intellects
and argue about high and holy matters. God condescends to
take part in the discussion. He knows our difficulties and
expects us to use our brains. When we have taken our doubts
and misgivings to him we feel better. The air is cleared. Like
Job, we say that God is greater than our hearts and we can
leave all in his hands.

44

The Psalms in Worship

O come, let us worship and fall down: and kneel before the
Lord our Maker. PSALM 95. 6.

SCHOLARS USED to make great efforts to settle the author-
ship and date of the Psalms, in the light of the allusions in

117

them. The information contained in the descriptions found at the head of the Psalms in the Bible version cannot give any real help, for it represents the guesses of scribes, who probably had no trustworthy traditions. In Old Testament times people thought of the book or the poem rather than the author, and freely used other men's works without thought of copyright; broadly speaking, books were originally anonymous, though editors would collect the writings of great men and ascribe them to the authors.

So to-day scholars prefer to ask about any given psalm, Why was it put in the Bible? and, because it got there in order to be used, On what occasions was it sung? Many of the psalms are very old, but the Psalter as we have it was compiled as the hymnbook of the Temple rebuilt after the Exile. We know that there were choirs of Levites and that song was extensively used. Some of the occasions suggested in modern books are very speculative, but others only need to be pointed out to become perfectly clear.

Let us then think of Psalm 95, the Venite, so familiar from its use in Mattins. It is obviously an invitation to worship. The congregation have assembled at some spot away from the Temple. They are invited to join in an act of worship. "O come, let us sing unto the Lord: let us heartily rejoice in the strength of our salvation." They move off, praising God for the bounty of creation. He made the dry land and the mountains, the sea and all the creatures therein. Whatever claims other nations may make, our God "is a great King above all gods". So they proceed, not ashamed to make a joyful noise. The Hebrews had no ideas of the niceties of modern musicians and would not have stopped to ask if they had trained voices. As we see from Psalm 150, their worship was as noisy as possible, with all the instruments they could get, to say nothing of the stamping of feet in dancing.

They now reach the gates of the Temple and, action accompanying words, they worship and fall down, kneeling

118

before the Lord their Maker. We should expect them to pass in, but no. They are met by a priest, probably accompanied by a choir, who gives a solemn warning. Acting as God's spokesman, he asks, Are you worthy? Are you better than your fathers in the wilderness, who put the Lord to the test? Israel is all one: if you inherit the faith of Abraham. you inherit the disobedience of the people of Moses' time, who hardened their hearts and grieved the Lord, who erred from my ways, so that they were shut out from the promised land.

Now we see the appropriateness of the psalm at the beginning of Sunday worship. At the height of our joy we are reminded of our unworthiness. The second half of the psalm is omitted sometimes, but has its special lesson.

Another example of a liturgical psalm is Psalm 24. Once more a procession winds its way up the hill of the Lord. The members remind themselves of the moral qualifications for entering the Temple. Only "he that hath clean hands and a pure heart . . . shall receive the blessing from the Lord". Once more they reach the gates and are met by the Temple choir, who challenged their right to enter. This time very ancient words are used, going back to the early days of Solomon's Temple, when the worshippers carried some visible symbol of the presence of God, such as the Ark. They cry, "Open the gates . . . and the King of glory shall come in". "Who is the King of glory?" rings out the challenge. "It is the Lord strong and mighty, even the Lord mighty in battle." We know that at one time the Hebrews used to take the Ark with them on their campaigns (see Num. 10. 35; 1 Sam. 4. 3). The challenge is repeated and answered in the same words. Then the guardians open the gates and the incomers pass in, filled with indescribable joy.

45

Help from the Sanctuary

Send thee help from the sanctuary. PSALM 20. 2.

THIS PSALM is a liturgy composed for the solemn moment when the king dedicates himself and his people to God before leading them out to war.

The choir begins: "The Lord hear thee in the day of trouble: the name of the God of Jacob defend thee." In praying for the king they pray for themselves, the nation whom the king represents. He has made the customary act of piety by coming to the Temple and knows that he has them behind him. "Send thee help from the sanctuary." He uses the means of grace as they were known in those days and offers sacrifices. So the choir pray that his offering may be accepted. "Remember all thy offerings: and accept thy burnt-sacrifice." The king's purpose is also the nation's—victory; so they can pray without misgivings: "Grant thee thy heart's desire: and fulfil all thy mind."

At this point the whole congregation lift up their voices and cry: "We will rejoice in thy salvation . . . the Lord perform all thy petitions."

Now we must suppose a pause. The priest in charge of the service receives an oracle from the unseen Lord, promising victory, which he delivers to the king, singing: "Now know I that the Lord helpeth his Anointed and will hear him from his holy heaven." We need not ask whether there was an element of wishful thinking in this conviction of success. It is sufficient to say that it was a sincere act of religion; if after all they were defeated, they would probably have said that God allowed a lying spirit to intervene (see 1 Kings 22. 22). Filled with confidence the king, identifying himself with his people, goes on: "Some put their trust in chariots, and some in horses: but we will remember the name of the Lord our God." The psalm ends with a shout from the whole congregation: "Save, Lord, and hear us, O King of heaven: when we call upon thee."

The world has grown old since then, and we have learned so much in long years of war that it would be difficult to use the psalm for the same purpose as that of the original worshippers. I suggest that it makes a beautiful prayer on behalf of the parish priest. You are always safe in praying for him as one experiencing "the day of trouble". A devoted priest is rarely free from trouble. When the souls of men and women are concerned, something is always going wrong, and in so far as he is conscientious he must feel pain. When faithful communicants lapse, when the newly confirmed drop off, when quarrels arise among Church people, then and on many other occasions sorrow afflicts the priest.

We shall always be in season when we pray that the priest may have strength from the sanctuary, that he may get spiritual food from the services of the Church, and especially from the sacrament of the altar; that God may remember all his prayers and fulfil his desire, the salvation of souls. The life of the parish depends so greatly on the priest that, when he is blessed and his prayers are answered, the whole congregation rejoices in his salvation.

Now we think of the secret place where God and his minister converse together and of the priest's answered prayer, and of his joy when he can say from experience: "Now know I that the Lord helpeth his Anointed and will hear him from his holy heaven." It is comparatively easy, at least in certain parishes, to achieve apparent success by concentrating on social activities, at the cost of neglecting spiritual things. So let us think of our parties and entertainments as the modern counterpart of chariots and horses and declare: "Some put their trust in chariots, and some in

121

horses: but we will remember the name of the Lord our God."

46

Recovery from Sickness

Thou hast turned my heaviness into joy.
PSALM 30. 11 (Prayer Book Version)

THE PROBLEM of sickness is always with us. The general level of health is higher than it used to be, thanks to medical skill, better and more balanced food, and above all modern sanitation. But few of us escape periodical illness and the resulting pains. Perhaps the lesson of helplessness and dependence on others is a necessary part of our training in this world. It would be rash to assume that sickness is always an evil.

But how much worse a trial must sickness have been in Old Testament times! A Hebrew suffered in his body as much as we do, if not more in the absence of alleviating medicines. But he had a mental trouble which we are spared, for it was generally held that illness was sent by God as a punishment for sin. The insight which Christians gain by contemplating the Cross and remembering that God's beloved Son suffered agonies, "though he had done no sin", was denied to him. On the other hand, when he recovered he had an intensity of happiness unknown to us; besides the return of vitality he had the consciousness of God's favour restored.

Psalm 30 is a poem describing how a healthy man was laid low by sickness and restored to health. We may suppose that the author was unusually gifted and that he composed these lovely verses: and that the priests wrote it down for use by other sufferers when they came to the Temple to give thanks for recovery. He begins with praise that his cry has been heard and God has not "made my foes to triumph over me". These foes may be personal enemies who rejoice at his troubles, but remembering the ideas of that age we guess that he thinks of witchcraft, sorcerers who have put the evil eye on him. "Thou hast brought my soul out of *hell*." *Sheol* is the Hebrew word; it means the underworld of the departed, which the devout looked upon with horror, for at this early period it suggested banishment from the Lord. A later psalm (139. 8) realizes that God is everywhere: "if I go down into hell (*Sheol*), thou art there also." The Hebrews often spoke of severe illness as a form of death. We can understand this when we think of the experience of unconsciousness. Waking up from a coma, a man would naturally think that he had gone down into *Sheol* and come back again. The psalmist then calls on his friends to rejoice with him. How wonderful is God's mercy: "Heaviness may endure for a night, but joy cometh in the morning"—a precious verse which we have often proved true.

He then reverts to his illness. "In my prosperity I said, I shall never be removed ." Especially when we are young and physically fit and feel on top of the world, this exactly describes our feelings at times. But the man who is always "fighting fit" is likely to trust in himself unduly and may be better for a spell of illness, teaching him to rely on God. The psalmist interpreted his illness as sent from God, a sign that God's face was turned away from him, and he did what we too often fail to do: "I gat me to my Lord right humbly." He pleaded with God. What good will it do if I go down into the pit and am no longer in this world to give thanks to God and declare his truth? One of the glories of Old Testament religion is the unselfish serving of God without hope of a reward in the next life. The psalmists' point of view is, "I must go to Church as much as possible now, I shan't be able to when I'm dead." Then our author goes on: "Hear,

O Lord, and have mercy upon me: Lord, be thou my helper."

His prayer is heard. "Thou hast turned my heaviness into joy . . . and girded me with gladness. Therefore shall every good man sing of thy praise without ceasing." This is indeed a lesson for us. The old rhyme runs thus:

> The devil was sick, the devil a monk would be;
> The devil was well, and the devil a monk he'd be.

The temptation is to resume our old life and forget our good resolutions. Let us rather, like the Hebrew psalmist, often think with gratitude of our periods of illness and thank God for his mercies.

47

Christ our High Priest

Thou art a priest for ever after the order of Melchisedek.
PSALM 110. 4; HEBREWS 5. 6.

ONE OF St Paul's great sayings is, "Christ is the end of the law . . . unto every one that believeth" (Rom. 10. 4). As we see from the Sermon on the Mount, Jesus, the Son of God, knew the Father's will in a way impossible for Moses, and so he proclaimed, "It was said to them of old time . . . but *I say unto you* . . .". At the same time he built on the foundation of the old Law, drawing out its full meaning, so we may say "Christ is the *completion* of the Law" rather than the end; but the meaning is much the same.

Now the Epistle to the Hebrews deals with another problem. The Law was largely concerned with priesthood and sacrifice—what happens to them? The answer is that the old priesthood has come to an end, for now we have one High Priest, Christ, who belongs not to the sacred tribe of Levi but to Judah. The old priesthood had to go, for by it a man was a priest simply because he was the son of his father. In the new High Priest everything we need is found. He is both Priest and Victim, for he offers his body in perfect obedience to the will of God.

The question next arises, Is there anything in the Old Testament to support this teaching? The writer finds what he wants in the mysterious figure of Melchisedek (Gen. 14), so great a man that even Abraham pays tithes to him. And he quotes Psalm 110, at which we must now look. This psalm was written to be sung at the Coronation of a king at Jerusalem, hardly David but more likely a later king of David's line. "The Lord said unto my Lord (the king), sit thou on my right hand, until I make thine enemies thy footstool." In the ancient East the death of a king often meant that subject kingdoms rebelled against his successor. So God promises to help the new sovereign. It is a curious thing that the old language lingers on to-day. If we generally omit "Confound their politics" we at least sing, "Send her victorious".

We shall see other parallels to our Coronation Service as we go on. The king has been enthroned, now he receives the sceptre, "the rod of thy power", as a symbol of authority. This we may call the Investiture with the insignia of royalty. Next "the people offer themselves willingly in the day of thy power", corresponding to the Acclamation in our service, when the Westminster boys shout *Vivat Rex* (or *Regina*), "Long live the King (or Queen)".

Then the king is ordained as a priest. The anthem beginning "Zadok the priest" keeps our service close to the Bible. We do not suppose that priestly power has been given to our monarch, but the solemnity of the Coronation contributes greatly to the reverence in which she is held. What sort of a priesthood is given to the Hebrew king? He is not of Aaron's line but carries on the privileges and duties of the old priest-kings of Jerusalem, of which Melchisedek was one. These include offering sacrifice, the idea being that, just as in primitive times the father of the family sacrificed, so now does the king as father of his people.

Finally, "He shall drink of the brook in the way: therefore shall he lift up the head". There is no passage in the Bible throwing light on this, so we are reduced to guessing. Jerusalem had one important well only, Gihon, now called the Virgin's spring, by the side of the brook Kidron. It was regarded as sacred, and the best explanation of the verse is that a cup of water was brought to the king, who drank it reverently and was refreshed in body and soul for his new task. You will remember that the climax of our Coronation service is the Holy Communion, when the Sovereign drinks the cup of the Lord.

This may sound fanciful, but it is to be expected that the root-ideas of our ages-old service should be drawn from the Bible. In conclusion, let us say a few words about Christian priesthood. Some people say that the Church has a ministry but no priests. There is only one Priest now, Christ Jesus; men to-day may be ministers, not priests. But if Christ is our Priest, then his Body the Church must be a priestly body. As St Peter says (2. 5): "Ye are to be a holy priesthood, to offer up spiritual sacrifices, acceptable to God through Jesus Christ." And a little later (verse 9): "Ye are a royal priesthood." If so, then the psalm put into the mouth of David the priest has lessons for us. The priests are the hands of the priestly body, a ministerial priesthood, deriving their honour from the Head of the Church. But, unlike the priesthood in ancient Israel, each man is called individually by Christ and answers, "Here am I, send me".

126

48

Vegetarianism

Daniel purposed in his heart that he would not defile himself
with the king's meat, nor with the wine which he drank.
DANIEL 1. 8.

THE FIRST chapter of Daniel tells us about four Jewish
pages at the court of Nebuchadnezzar king of Babylon
(Daniel, Shadrach, Meshach, and Abednego), who refused to
eat meat or drink wine. The chamberlain in charge of them
was distressed. The king liked to see the youths about the
court looking healthy and when he saw these boys pining
away would vent his displeasure on *him*. However, the
experiment was tried and the boys were fed on vegetarian
food and water with the result that they surpassed all their
companions in health, to say nothing of their intellectual
achievements.

It would be too simple an explanation to say that the Bible
here teaches us to avoid meat and abstain from alcohol; if we
are to understand the passage we must consider the background of the book of Daniel.

About 165 years before Christ the Jews suffered a severe
persecution at the hands of their ruler, the Syrian king
Antiochus Epiphanes; the story is told in the first book of
Maccabees. Antiochus was beset with political difficulties
owing to the pressure of the Romans. Burdened by a war
indemnity, he decided that the Jews must contribute their
share to the expenses of the State from the treasures stored in
the Temple at Jerusalem. They said that the treasures were
under the protection of God and it was sacrilege to use them
for such a purpose. For financial and other reasons Antiochus
determined to tighten up the organization of his great empire,
which stretched eastward to the border of India; only if it was

unified with one official religion could it have a chance against Rome. There was no objection to local religions, so long as everybody recognized Olympian Zeus as the supreme God. Some of the Jews, not all, thought this was apostasy and resisted, and persecution broke out. The actual occasion of civil war was when one family refused to take part in the sacrificial feast ordered by the king. This was considered an act of rebellion and disloyalty.

Now why was this so wrong in their eyes? The meat had been offered to idols, and by eating it they would be guilty of idolatry. And at heathen feasts a libation of wine was made. This meant that the cup was shaken and a few drops were spilled before the image of a heathen god. Perhaps we think that the Jews were narrow-minded and might have made a small concession in the interests of peace. But they felt they must be loyal to their convictions and concede nothing. The writer of the book of Daniel had their needs in view. By telling the story of a hero who even in the king's palace refused to go against his conscience he meant to inspire them to hold out.

There used to be a temperance hymn beginning, "Dare to be a Daniel"; that is, dare, like Daniel in the story, to stand out against public opinion and abstain from alcoholic drinks. That of course is not what the Bible story means. Not wine in itself *but the king's wine* was refused, wine that was connected with idolatry. The moral of the story is not vegetarianism or teetotalism but constancy in persecution.

The issue is raised again in the New Testament, especially at Corinth, where Christians asked whether they could eat flesh bought in the market, knowing that it had been killed ceremonially in connection with heathen temples. St Paul's teaching is wise and clear (see 1 Cor. 8). On the one hand, he says, an idol is nothing, there are no gods other than the God of the Christians; nothing has happened to the meat, which is God's creation, at which he looked and saw it to be good. Those who can appreciate this truth he calls "the strong" (see Rom. 14 and 15. 1). They may eat and do no wrong. But there is another side to the question. Many Christians cannot rise to this height but feel that real defilement is incurred by eating such meat. St Paul calls them "the weak". Weak though they are, their prejudices must be respected. The strong must bear the infirmities of the weak. For himself, "if meat make my brother to stumble, I will eat no flesh for evermore".

Jesus said to his disciples: "Eat such things as are set before you" (Luke 10. 8). On your missionary journeys accept gratefully what your hosts provides. Don't ask whether all the rules of the Rabbis have been kept. This surely must be our general rule to-day. No food defiles a man; in the nature of the case it cannot, and our conduct must be dictated by good manners and common sense. The scientific view is that man is an omnivorous animal, able to adapt himself to many kinds of food, including flesh; our teeth prove that. Neither religion nor science tells us to be vegetarians. Many, however, have a tender conscience in regard to the slaughter of animals to provide them with food and like to reduce their consumption of meat to a minimum, if not to avoid it completely. We should honour their consciences. As regards alcoholic liquors it is harder to decide. Fermentation is a natural process, and we cannot say that the use of alcohol is wrong in itself. But excessive use of it does so much harm, especially in causing accidents, that the utmost moderation is required of Christians. Teetotalism is out of fashion to-day, but some people at least ought to abstain in order to make it easier for the weaker brethren.

49

The Son of Man

I saw in the night visions, and behold there came with the clouds of heaven one like unto a son of man, and he came to the ancient of days. DANIEL 7. 13.

THE BACKGROUND of Daniel's visions is the life and death struggle of the Jews with their foreign overlord Antiochus Epiphanes, about 165 years before Christ. They were fighting for liberty to practise their religion. You can read about the war in the books of Maccabees, in the Apocrypha. They give the actual events, but Daniel shows us the intense faith that nerved the Jews for their struggle. The writer looks out on the the world and sees the hand of God in history, in the rise and fall of empires. In this seventh chapter he has a vision of four kingdoms: first Babylon, depicted as a lion; then the Medes and Persians, as a bear and a leopard; then the fourth beast, which has no animal's name but is the worst of all. This last is the Syrian kingdom of Antiochus.

The curtain falls on these events of history and rises for the final scene of judgement. The Ancient of Days, the eternal God, sits on his throne, and "one like unto a son of man" is brought before him; and to him is given universal dominion.

Now "son of man" is the Hebrew way of saying "man", as we see from the psalm: "What is man, that thou art mindful of him: and the son of man that thou visitest him?" (Psalm 8. 4). We have the idiom elsewhere in the Bible: "sons of Belial" means "wicked men", and James and John for their impetuosity are called by Jesus "sons of thunder". Later in the chapter the Son of Man is explained as "the saints of the Most High"; dominion and victory are to be given to the godly party in Israel.

If this was the sense of the vision when it was first written down, it is far from exhausting the meaning, which is different in other places. "Son of Man" is used constantly in the book of Ezekiel, on the lips of a heavenly being addressing the prophet, and carries with it the suggestion of a representative man who stands for his people. In the book of Enoch, parts of which were written about the same time as Daniel, the Son of Man is the Messiah in heaven waiting for the time of his manifestation.

The original meaning in Daniel, then, is that the time of the great beasts, or world-powers, is coming to an end; the law of the jungle will not always prevail, but will be succeeded by a human or humane régime, which will last for ever. How passionately we desire this when we feel depressed by the wars and political convulsions of the twentieth century! But for Christians this first meaning is overshadowed when they remember that their Saviour chose "Son of Man" as the way in which he described himself.

"Son of Man" was chosen by Jesus because it was so full of meaning; it partly revealed and partly concealed his claims. We must interpret it in the light of the Old Testament, from which we learn three lessons.

First, the Son of God is fully human. Jesus thought of himself as man, the perfect Son, "knowing his Father's mind completely and doing his will in all things. Those who study the Gospel closely are free from the danger of thinking of Jesus as God thinly veiled under the outward appearance of humanity.

Secondly, Jesus, though he was an individual man, is representative man in a sense none of us can be. He sums up the strivings of all the ages and, as we know from the achievements of missions, is the universal Saviour. Men of all races and cultures find in him the fulfilment of all their needs and longings.

Thirdly, "Son of Man" teaches us to find Jesus at the end as well as in the past. Whatever advances in scientific dis-

131

covery and technology the world may witness, the secret of living as sons of God and in harmony with our fellow-men is to be learned from him alone. We shall always be going back to him as the source of life and the inspiration of conduct. And when the world-process is brought to an end and God's judgement is passed on men and their achievements, that judgement will be pronounced by the eternal Son of God, who has lived our life and shared our sufferings.

50

Wisdom and Folly

Wisdom is better than rubies; and all the things that may be desired are not to be compared unto her. PROVERBS 8. 11.

THERE IS no reason to doubt the tradition that the book of Proverbs goes back to Solomon, who, we are told, "spake of trees, from the cedar that is in Lebanon even unto the hyssop that springeth out of the wall; he spake also of beasts, and of fowl, and of creeping things, and of fishes" (1 Kings 4. 33). This suggests that Hebrew proverbs at first were not exactly religious, a conclusion borne out by the modern discovery that some part of Proverbs came from Egypt. This is just what we should expect, since Solomon married Pharaoh's daughter, who must have brought Egyptian ideas with her. The Egyptian collections of proverbs were meant to be used in schools, to teach boys how to behave when they grew up and had posts under Government; and Solomon too had a well-organized empire needing a Civil Service. The Greeks, who were philosophers, produced great men like Socrates and Plato: the Hebrews, being practical people, preferred homely teaching about everyday life. But philosophy and proverbs were two different days of understanding the same thing—the world in which we live.

Let me quote some familiar sayings. "In vain is the net spread in the sight of any bird" (Prov. 1. 17). "In the multitude of counsellors there is safety" (11. 14). "Hope deferred maketh the heart sick" (13. 12). "A soft answer turneth away wrath" (15. 1). "Pride goeth . . . before a fall" (16. 18). "Answer a fool according to his folly (26. 5). "Faithful are the wounds of a friend" (27. 6). Such verses have become part of the English language. Then how witty are some of the proverbs! "It is naught, it is naught, saith the buyer. And when he is gone his way, then he boasteth" (20. 14). Or we may quote the sluggard's excuse for lying in bed, "There is a lion in the way" (26. 13).

Proverbs as a whole represents what we may call natural religion; there is nothing about the chosen people, or the covenant, or the expected Messiah and his kingdom. Rather, we have the practical wisdom which is more or less the same for all nations. Proverbs seems hard-hearted sometimes. The fool is always condemned; there is no, "Poor chap, I'm sorry for him". It is a hard world, but it must have been bracing and have produced strong characters. There is no flattery of the "little man" as in our popular press to-day. The motive is prudential: be good and you will have a long and happy life. The hope of a world to come seems not to have been revealed.

Now we might wonder why such a book is in the Bible and in what sense we can call it inspired, until we come to chapter 8, where the most glorious vista opens out. Folly is blamed: wisdom, its opposite, is praised. But what is wisdom? It is the practical good sense with which we meet the trials of every day life. Where does it come from? Its origin is divine. It is the inspiring force of God's universe. And so in chapter 8 it praises are sung. It is that which holds the State together. "By me (wisdom) kings reign, and princes decree justice." It comes from above. "The Lord formed me

133

in the beginning of his way, before his works of old. I was set up from everlasting, from the beginning, or even the earth was . . . When he established the heavens, I was there . . . Then I was with him, as a master workman, and I was daily his delight, rejoicing always before him . . . Whoso findeth me findeth life, and shall obtain favour of the Lord." Then in the next chapter (the ninth) Lady Wisdom is personified. She invites all to come to her house and partake of her feast. "Come, eat ye of my bread, and drink of the wine which I have mingled." But there is another voice calling, that of Lady Folly, who also stands at her door and bids men come in. Many go in, knowing not "that the dead are there: that her guests are in the depths of hell".

So this book of the Bible, which at first seemed to fall below the level of an inspired book, proves to teach a noble lesson. All our monotonous tasks may be inspired by the divine Worker of Creation. He who made the stars needs our co-operation. We can keep his laws as we do our work in factory, field, office, or house, and contribute our mite to the carrying out of the purposes of Creation. God who made the world continues to uphold it and invites us to be his fellow-workers.

51

Is Life worth Living?

Vanity of vanities, all is vanity. ECCLESIASTES 1. 2.

IS LIFE worth living? The author of Ecclesiastes answers, No. His reflections are put in the mouth of Solomon, the famous king of old who had everything man could desire and found it "vanity of vanities". Wealth and high position brought no lasting pleasure but only boredom. Even the pursuit of wisdom caused grief and sorrow. Then he tried mirth and folly with the same result. He concluded that wisdom and folly came to the same thing in the end; perhaps eating and drinking is the only satisfactory pleasure: "Who can eat . . . more than I?" (2. 25).

Now why should this be? Apparently a man's life is predestinated, fixed by fate. The wheel of fortune is going round all the time and eventually comes back to where it started: "there is no new thing under the sun" (1. 9); progress is impossible. A man's birth is fixed, so is his death. He does all things in turn: planting and plucking up, weeping and laughing, going to war and making peace.

Suppose he turns from his own fate to that of others. He has only to look at the law-courts and their injustice to see what a grim time the average man has. This is God's doing, to abase us and show us that we are worth no more than beasts. "That which befalleth the sons of men befalleth beasts . . . man hath no pre-eminence above the beasts (3. 19). Some suggest that there is a difference for the spirit of man goes upward at death, but "who knows?" (3. 21).

Then Ecclesiastes considers the practice of religion—what good does that do? "Keep thy foot when thou goest to the house of God (probably meaning, Remove thy sandals); for to draw nigh to hear is better than to give the sacrifice of fools: for they know not that they do evil" (5. 1). Sacrifices are useless, there is something to be said for listening to lectures or sermons. Certainly you should not worry over the details of the law: "Be not righteous overmuch . . . why shouldest thou destroy thyself?" (7. 16). Again, the old delight in having property to leave in your will disappears when you have no son. If you want pleasure, go to a funeral, not to a wedding (7. 2).

The lowest rung of the ladder of despair is reached when the writer says (9. 5): "The living know that they shall die (they have that satisfaction): but the dead know not anything (not even the joy of knowing they will die)."

Well, in conclusion, make the most of youth, you are only young once. "Rejoice, O young man in thy youth . . . remove sorrow from my heart" (11. 9). Make the most of youth while it lasts. Old age is coming, when the bright dawn is suceeded by clouds and darkness. The arms become weak and the knees tremble, the gums are toothless ("the grinders cease because they are few"), the eyes grow dim, you become deaf and cannot hear music properly, you sleep badly at night and the birds wake you up, you cannot walk up hill. For "man goeth to his long home, and the mourners go about the streets" (12. 5). A wonderful picture of old age without the blessings of false teeth, spectacles, and hearing aids, things which enable us to keep human to the last but which we take for granted.

This then is the main argument of the book—how did it get into the Bible? Because by the side of all the pessimism there is much sound teaching of a different kind, telling of God's judgement on sinners and proclaiming that the whole duty of man is to "fear God and keep his commandments" (12. 13). The book was too attractive to be lost and it may be that an editor revised it to contradict the teachings where necessary and, if it was dangerous, to give the antidote.

Or, and this is a more attractive explanation, the author was in two minds and lets us see the different moods through which he passed. Thus he said, "Rejoice, O young man, in thy youth", and himself added, "For all these things God will bring thee unto judgement", and, "Remember thou thy Creator in the days of thy youth". Let us suppose that this is the right solution. Then what a wonderful book Ecclesiastes is! Here is a man who sounded the depths of despair and decided that life is bad, not good: pleasures turn to ashes in our mouth. But nevertheless he will not give up faith in God. Like Job he says, "Though he slay me, yet will I put my trust in him". The book celebrates a miracle of faith. All has failed me—riches, wisdom, pleasure of all kinds. The practice of religion has nothing to offer me. Youth is over, a cheerless old age is before me. In spite of all I believe in God. Is it not worth while having such a book in the Bible?

52

Earthly and Heavenly Love

I am my beloved's, and my beloved is mine.
SONG OF SONGS 6. 3.

THE HEBREWS were men of like passions with ourselves, and love-making played its part in their lives. So we should guess from various stories in the Old Testament. That they loved so passionately and brought so much romance into their wooing we should not know if it were not for one book, the Song of Songs. It is a book that overflows with delight in the beauty of Nature and of all created things, including human bodies. Let us look at some passages. "He brought me to the banqueting house, and his banner over me was love" (2. 4). "Rise up, my fair one, and come away. For, lo, the winter is past, the rain is over and gone; the flowers appear on the earth; the time of the singing of birds is come, and the voice of the turtle-dove is heard in our land" (2. 10-12).

Well, the average Hebrew girl, poor thing, must have had a hard life, marrying at 15 or so and having many babies, besides the care of the house. But for a brief period she had her moments of enchantment, when she was a queen to her boy friend and with complete frankness returned his passion. This is one of the surprises of the book, the innocent way in which the girl reciprocates the man's love. Hebrew girls were by no means Victorian in their outlook, indeed they were frankly modern. The woman in our book says: "My beloved is white and ruddy, the chiefest among ten thousand . . . His mouth is most sweet: yea, he is altogether lovely. This is my beloved, and this is my friend, O daughters of Jerusalem" (5. 10, 16).

We have here, then, an interesting piece of social history, but, as in the case of some other books, we are inclined to ask how the Song got into the Bible. Courting and love-making are part of human nature and cannot, indeed ought not to, be suppressed. But on the other hand they do not need to be encouraged.

First, we can be sure of one thing. The Jews who valued the book sufficiently to put it into the Bible never dreamed of anything but legitimate married love, leading to children. "He maketh the barren woman to keep house, and to be a joyful mother of children", says the Psalm (113. 9); motherhood was regarded as the greatest possible privilege and joy. Women generally were expected to keep in the background and be subordinate to men. But when they became mothers of sons, their status was recognized and they were honoured and exercised great influence. The king's mother, for example, is often mentioned in the books of Kings as a person of importance. In Proverbs the father and the mother are often mentioned as being entitled to equal honour. So the Jews who so esteemed marriage approved of the love songs that preceded marriage.

But this would not have sufficed to make the Song of Songs a religious book. When the Rabbis, about A.D. 100, fixed the limits of the Old Testament, they interpreted our book as an allegory of the divine love which God has for Israel. This was a bold step, but they did not go further than the prophet Hosea had gone long ago. The first three chapters of his book actually depict God as the husband of an unfaithful wife, who is very patient with her and after a period of probation takes her back, meaning that Israel has fallen into idolatry but, if

138

she repents, will be pardoned and restored to her former place of honour.

The question remains, can we legitimately use the Song of Songs of the love which Christ has for his Church? And, if so, can we fill out the details from the verses of the Song? St Paul seems to answer the question. "Christ loved the Church, and gave himself up for it . . . that he might present the Church to himself a glorious Church, not having spot or wrinkle or any such thing" (Eph. 5. 25, 27). He does not go into details and certainly does not encourage us to apply the allegory to the individual soul. We can hardly say that it ought not to be so applied, in view of the use made of the book by masters of the spiritual life, such as St Bernard of Clairvaux, and the well known verses of popular hymns, such as "Jesu, lover of my soul". But this form of devotion suits a limited number of people, and then only when they have made some progress in the spiritual life under wise direction.